Paracetamol

Shirley +

Animal Tales
And
Funny Stories

Dedication

To all our pets past, present and future.

Contents

The House that I grew up in

Animals! I have always loved them. They share our lives as companions, giving us much joy and funny moments. They even seem to pick up our moods and share our good times as well as the bad. What makes all the following stories so remarkable, with one exception (A Magical Story) is that they are all true and the animals were and are all real characters. There are some people stories too, funny moments with family or neighbours but most of the stories are about our four-legged friends.

Faithful Friends

We always had dogs when I was growing up, usually two at once. Each dog had its own individual character. There was gentle Jenny, a white Bull Terrier, she did not have much brain, Simon an intelligent black Dachshund, Perry another dachshund or Pooky for short and Henry the loveable Bassett Hound who, when he was a puppy, used to stand on his own floppy ears and sometimes get a bit stuck and would have to be rescued. We used to get some looks when he was walked round the village. Then there was barmy

Barney, another Dachshund, who one day eat a sherry glass! We were sitting in the lounge chatting and I put my sherry glass down on the floor. The next thing we were aware of was loud crunching noises. Heavens! He has eaten the glass! It did not seem to affect him though.

Every Christmas we had a cousin of Dad's come to stay. He was called Uncle Charles. He used to write little poems and this is what he wrote about Perry.

> There was a young dachshund called Perry
> Who said, "I become after sherry
> Forgetful and thinner
> Because for my dinner,
> I can't find the bones that I bury."

Perhaps this little ditty is more appropriate for Barmy Barney!

Ours was a beautiful rambling old house in a small village in Northamptonshire. The golden coloured walls were two feet thick and half the roof was thatched. This made my Dad very nervous on bonfire night and he would pace up and down anxiously keeping an eye on the night sky. There were two front doors because at one time it had been split into two dwellings. The dogs lived at the front of the house, the kitchen end, while Tigger, our wild tabby cat lived at the back. The main door had a thatched porch and led into a large hall where a grandfather clock ticked and chimed away the hours. At the other end of the house where Tigger lived the converted stable had been made into a sun room. Tigger's domain was the large back garden which used to be an orchard. Several small apple trees remained and one Victoria plum tree and those plums off that tree were deliciously sweet and juicy. There was also a huge vegetable patch, a deserted henhouse and a pigsty. A large barn was used as a garage and above this was the forbidden loft. It was forbidden because the floor was unsafe as there were a number of holes in the thin old floor boards.

In many ways it was a house of mystery. There was the small room above what used to be the old stable. It had no windows and could only be reached by a ladder from the outside. I remember the musty dusty smell when the door was opened and you peered into the gloom. It was just below this door that we used to carve our initials into the soft sandy stone. Some of the dates stretched across two centuries.

I was fascinated by the blocked up cellars. All that was left of them was a small grid set in the outside wall below the dining room window. Then there was the small cupboard door above the kitchen worktops and below the normal kitchen cupboards. This had a lovely brass knob and when opened you could peer through the cupboard that opened out into the lobby by the kitchen door.

My realm was the attic. I would play for hours under the knobbly hefty beams that stretched under the musty old thatch. You could hear all the sounds of the village up there as clear as anything.

At night in my bedroom it was very dark as the street lights were far away. I was scared of the dark for it felt very dense indeed in the old house. I would creep out of bed and draw back the thick velvet curtains and allow a streak of night light in. Sometimes in the middle of the night the oak stairs would creak for no reason.

In the winter time I would wake up to see frosty pictures on the inside of the window panes. I would sit on the cold tiles of the deep window sill and trace the lacy patterns with my fingers.

One of my earliest memories from that time was visiting the local butcher. Mum did most of her shopping from the local village store. Back in those days, in the early sixties, there were no big super markets, well not out in the sticks where we lived. We used to walk over to the other side of the village where the local butcher had a shop. While Mum was inside buying what we needed, I would go out the back where the pigs and chickens lived. I was thrilled to be allowed to feed the chickens. I would hold out my hand and they would come running from all directions and their hard little beaks would peck at the food, tickling my palms. But the pigs were my favourite. They seemed rather large or perhaps I was rather small. They loved having their backs scratched. This involved having a large stick and rubbing it gently up and down their rough hairy backs. Clouds of dust would rise up into the air and they would grunt with pleasure. What a treat. My father loved pigs and I suppose I get my love of pigs from him. He used to tell me this little gem of wisdom:

> Dogs look up to you
> Cats look down
> But pigs look equal.

Henry the Bassett Hound was adorable but always getting into mischief. For one thing he

kept digging holes in the flower bed. Another time I had cooked steaks for myself and Dad. I had left tea ready on the table and went to call Dad. I was only away for a moment. When I came back the steak was gone and there was Henry under the table licking his chops. More things he got up to are recorded in 'Letters from my Dad' at the end of the book.

Tigger, our puss, came to us by accident. Simon the Dachshund was out in the front garden and got very excited about something under the oil tank. When we went to investigate, we discovered a very scared ferocious tabby kitten. So Tigger came to live with us but she always kept her distance and was not particularly friendly. One funny incident I recall was when I was sitting in the lounge watching telly. Suddenly Tigger burst into the room, ran up to me, patted me on the cheek and ran off again. Such was the extent of her affection!

We were very fond of her although the feeling did not seem mutual and one day, while sitting in the back garden enjoying the summer sun and gazing out onto the pond and sea of snapdragons, my sister and I composed a poem. It is not a particularly good poem but it captures the nature of our puss.

The Mad Cat

A cat have we
Who sailed up tree
And there she sat
Our head to bat
Upon a branch
That did by chance
O'er hang the grass
On which we pass.
This cat she can
If she doth plan
To make you fright
At her ferocious sight
With her tail abush
And her claws uptight
Her eyes aflame
She looks insane.
From the tree doth leap
To land in a heap
Lifts herself up
With a dignified air
And casts upon us
A contemptuous stare
With a terrible gleam in her eye
She dances sideways by!

One story about Tigger sticks in my mind. My Mum was a wonderful cook. Her pastry melted in your mouth and her apple pies were famous within the family. She could also make beautiful cakes. She used to run the cake stall for the local church fete every year and a few days before the event, she would bake lots of cakes. They were all different, Victoria sponge, coffee cake, orange cake, lemon cake and chocolate cake. They would all be decorated to perfection in different ways and sometimes she would roll the sides in ground nuts.

Our dining room table was a large one, a relic from Dad's past. It was made of mahogany and if one squinted and peered over the surface in a certain light, you could just about discern the history of England when Mum and I had inadvertently written on its soft surface while Mum was helping me with my studies. All the cakes would be spread out all over the table and the doors to the dining room were kept shut.

However, one year Tigger managed to get in. Right in the middle of the table was a beautiful chocolate cake oozing with butter cream icing. Imagine our horror when we came down in the morning to find that the chocolate cake had a complete and perfect circle of icing missing from the middle! She must have spent all night licking up the glorious chocolate. Funnily enough, nothing else was touched. Such is the mysterious ways of cats!

Ours was not the only old house in the village. Just behind us and set back from the road was another golden stoned large house. An old lady lived there and I was allowed to visit. Like our house it had two front doors so I suppose it had been two houses at one time.

What really fascinated me was that it had two staircases as well. One led up from the hall and the other one led up from the kitchen. The staircase leading up from the kitchen was reached through an old latched door and was uncarpeted. The room upstairs was not used for living in but in the autumn it would have the wonderful smell of stored apples which had been picked from the huge orchard at the back. The kitchen also had a strange little tunnel set in the thick wall and was about waist high. If you looked into it you could see the tunnel sloping down away from you and the hall was visible through the other end. I suppose it was used to send food down to the dining room which was on the other side of the hall.

My parents eventually moved down to Devon and lived in another old place but this time it was a cottage. There was oak panelling on some of the walls and a beautiful large log fire place in the lounge (or the drawing room as our Mum used to insist on calling it.) Another amusing incident

that happened there concerns Henry the Bassett Hound. Henry was always getting into trouble. Mum had been busy making bread that day and the bread dough had been left by the log fire to prove. Somehow Henry had managed to stroll in and eat the lot! Poor dog, he rolled over and could not move for a couple of hours.

There are perhaps more stories that could be told but for now let us move on to our feline friends.

Cats with Personalities

Dining Out

When we moved to Somerset our first cat was called Chester and was a large black and white tom. I wanted him to be called Spingo after a Cornish beer that we liked but it was not to be. No one could come up with something suitable so he was named after a horse I knew. A friend down the road called their cat Chester – short for chest of drawers. Cats should have many names, and Chester had many middle ones, Felix, Spingo, greedy guts....

He would be out all day but was always prompt for his meal times. Then mysteriously his pattern changed. He occasionally missed the odd meal and then would turn up for the next one. We were highly suspicious. There is nothing more annoying than someone else feeding the family pet. I put a collar on him but it did not seem to make much difference.

I knew he was not going very far away and decided to follow him. If anyone has ever tried to follow their cat you will appreciate that this is not an easy feat. Cats do not go the same routes as us. They often take the high ground over garden fences, walls and sometimes roofs and then they

go through private gardens skirting shrubs and meandering through flower beds. They just go different ways to us. I remember on one occasion I looked out of our landing window to see Chester on the roof admiring the view and the birds! He got up there by jumping up onto the roof of the extension which was only one storey high.

I waited for the chance to follow him. After giving him his tea one day, Chester decided he was off and made for the gardens at the back. I rushed off down the road to watch him emerge on the lane below. He then crossed the main road through the village. Presumably because he was black and white and moved like a mini zebra crossing, he had escaped death on numerous occasions. As I carried on watching from a safe and hidden distance, he then squeezed himself through a black iron gate and to my utter amazement, proceeded to rub noses with the dog who lived there! I had never seen him with a dog before so this was a new experience for me and they were obviously on good speaking terms.

I then went home to decide on a plan of action. Perhaps if I spoke to the owner all would be well. Eventually I did manage to have a chat with the lady who lived there.

"Oh!" she said. "I didn't realise he was owned by anyone. I thought he was a stray. Then he turned up with a collar."

A stray! Yeah right, I thought.

I had hoped that would be an end to the matter but no, he was still missing meals and sometimes days would go by without a glimpse of our family puss. Well I decided to take some serious action. I went round to the place where he was dining out and put a very brief but polite note on the door.

Please don't feed our cat. We've had him since he was a kitten and we're very fond of him.

I got home and within an hour I had a phone call.

"I would never dream of feeding somebody else's cat etc. etc."

I did not lose my temper and kept very calm and said,"Oh I'm very pleased to hear that!" Needless to say the note did the trick. She stopped giving him the odd meal and he returned to his usual pattern and that was that!

Felix, The Escape Artist

I stroke his long, smooth, ginger back.

"Ah! How he purrs! What a beautiful puss you are."

Felix is the friendliest cat I have ever known. He has four white feet, a white bib and a stripy

ginger white tail which he carries with dignity. His green eyes follow you round the room and he enjoys sharing our space. His squeak of a meow rather lets him down but at least he will not be littering the neighbourhood with his offspring. But there is a story attached to him. This cat has a history and I would like to share it with you.

We were given two beautiful ginger cats, brothers, called Leo and Felix. Leo was the great hunter and spent a lot of time outdoors. Felix was the timid one and he ruled indoors. On their arrival, we locked the cat flap so that we could keep them indoors and get them used to us and their new surroundings. What we did not know was that Felix was an escape artist.

The first night all was well and in the morning, we still had two cats. However, Felix had not been idle and all night had examined the cat flap thoroughly and had tried to make his bid for freedom. The next evening, he succeeded. Fortunately my husband came into the kitchen just in time to catch sight of Felix's ginger tail slipping through the cat flap. Quick as a flash, my husband rushed out onto the patio and lunged for the escaping puss but he was away, over the fence and gone.

We spent days trying to find him. Armed with a tin bowl, spoon and cat treats, we went out at 'cat time'. We have it on good authority that this is usually around 9pm in the summer. So, banging the tin bowl and feeling rather foolish, we stalked the back gardens and vegetable patches nearby and called in hushed voices,

"Felix" and "Here puss, puss." Alas, nothing. He really had scarpered.

After a few more days we had to admit defeat and that was that. It was about this time I had a dream. I was convinced that Felix would come back to us. In my dream, I stood at the front door and saw Felix at the top of the drive. He desperately wanted to come home but was prevented by a large, friendly dog. Nobody believed my dream but I felt it was a positive sign. I was convinced that he was living somewhere in the village and felt quietly

confident that one day, he would return. So time went on and a year passed.

We decided to get another cat and Meg arrived on the scene. Now we were back to two cats. Meg is a tabby fluffball and goes by many names, Megapuss, Powderpuff, Meg when she's in a good mood and Smeg when she is all teeth and claws and growls when she is picked up.

One miserable, wet, dark, winter evening, we lost Leo. He simply disappeared. He was there for breakfast as usual and then never showed for tea. He simply vanished into thin air, never to be seen again. It is always tragic when the family pet goes missing and you have no idea what has happened to them. Imagination can play dreadful tricks as you play out horrendous scenarios in your head. A faithful companion has gone and there is a vacuum left. Every time you hear the rattle of the cat flap, you rush into the kitchen with expectation only to find it is the other cat. As the days go by, hope diminishes and resignation sets in. So sad. It was not the same with Felix. We were barely past the formal introductions in his case.

It was not very long after this that we got a phone call from the vets.

"We've got a cat here that's registered to you. Are you prepared to pay the bill?"

"Oh, is that Leo?"

"No, it's Felix."

"Are you sure? We've recently lost Leo."

"Yes quite sure."

So feeling a bit puzzled, we agreed to pay the bill and talk to the people who had brought him in.

What had happened is this. Felix had been living at the top end of the village with an old man in one of the bungalows. When the old man had needed to go into a care home, Felix was left to fend for himself. He had lived rough for a few months and some people across the road had been feeding him. They had given him the name 'Paddy Paws' because he was so friendly and when he was picked up, would knead your chest enthusiastically. Then he had got himself into a scrap and needed a vet job. He was automatically scanned and they found that Felix had been chipped. His rescuers did not want to keep him because they already had three cats and a dog. To our delight when we went up to see him and to discover,

'Yes. It was definitely Felix!' We scooped him up, took him away and shut him in the lounge. He calmly looked at us and within the hour, he just sat down and purred. He was finally home.

We were so scared of losing him again that we did not let him out for a few days and yes, we did barricade the cat flap. However, we need not have worried. The first day we let him out, he would not go! He was terrified! I tried to

encourage him to go out and explore the great outdoors, so picked him up and made for the door. He was having none of it! He squirmed and wriggled in my arms and as soon as his feet touched the ground, he ran straight back in. Eventually it was Meg who enticed him to go out. He followed her out one day and all was well.

He is now very settled and the only clue to his life on the streets and his seedy past was when I went upstairs one day and caught him trying to drink from the toilet! Such is life!

Like all cats, he has quite a personality and one little incident that I would like to share with you concerns hot stuff. He apparently has a taste for curry. One day our freezer had decided to pack up. We managed to salvage most of the contents and left on the table was a packet of incredibly hot chilli sausages. We had only left the room for a moment when, coming back in, we were greeted with the sight of Felix helping himself to one of the sausages! The next day when Felix came back in, my husband, who had been robbed of his spicy feast, remarked sadistically, "Did it burn at both ends my puss?"

And you may wonder what the twist is to this tale. Well, believe it or not, it is all completely true. Sometimes it is the true stories that are the most remarkable.

Felix is the cat featured on the cover of this book.

Leo the Great Hunter

Leo, Felix's furry brother, was a big ginger tom, and was the outdoor type. He was also a great hunter. There was the time when I opened the kitchen door to be greeted by Leo carrying a massive rat (with Meg our young tabby kitten in hot pursuit) about to negotiate the cat flap with his prize. Needless to say, he was not allowed.

Then on another occasion I saw him lumbering up the patio steps dragging a live partridge by the neck. Meg was very interested. I am afraid our son had to deal with that one.

The previous week it had been the Lesser Spotted Woodpecker – must have been a young one. What an education our young Meg was getting! Leo is one of the softest, loveable cats you could ever know indoors but out in the garden jungle he is a beast. Whatever will he turn up with next?

We love spending time down in Cornwall and try and go down once a year. One of our favourite pubs is positioned close to the sea near to St. Agnes on the north coast. It is a very cosy pub and has not changed much over the years. It specialises in fresh local food and one board features a *Catch of the Day*.

One can just imagine Leo's menu:

Catch of the Day

Fresh mouse, exotic rat,
wild partridge,
colourful woodpecker,
half a snowy rabbit.....

Meg

After Felix disappeared, we decided to get another cat. Meg was still a very young kitten when we first had her. Her eyes were bright blue and she was a soft tabby fluff ball that could almost fit into the palm of your hand. She lived in the lounge which did not do much good to our leather furniture as the more she grew, the more energetic she became and left claw marks everywhere. She would cuddle up on my husband's chest and even as an adult, she would still cuddle up with him. Suddenly with no warning she would jump up, stay awhile and then be off.

As she grew, the first thing we noticed was her tail. It had been the size of a baby sweetcorn, but then it started to grow into a long haired plume with a cat attached. She had little black legs that make her look like she was wearing slinky black boots. She had a lot of energy and when coming in from the garden, would take a flying leap through the cat flap, streak through the kitchen and run up the stairs like a little furry elephant.

Helpful motto – know where your kitten is at all times! Her favourite activities were climbing up the curtains, trying to catch the washing through the window in the door, sliding along the kitchen floor in a shopping bag or baiting Uncle Leo. Leo would put up with it for so long and

then 'biff' she was floored. She also enjoyed 'bouncing' you round the corners and taking you by surprise. Good thing we were ready! Teatime. Make sure both cats get fed at exactly the same time otherwise Meg will be very slim and Leo will be very fat. One day after washing my hair I managed to freak out the kitten by wrapping my hair in a towel/turban. It took her weeks to accept this as normal. Another time I caught her on the kitchen worktop gazing at her own reflection in the shiny kettle.

"The conservatory is full of wonders for her," says our youngest. "She chases sunlight and shadows."

One day my husband was working away in his study, surrounded by paperwork and boxes. Suddenly he hears a rustle, looks up and sees nothing but a plume of a tail sticking up above the sea of boxes. Meg is always finding new places to sleep. In our younger son's room, I found her asleep on our son's secret stash of dirty underwear! I had wondered why underpants did not come through the wash very often! One of those forgotten but essential chores.

Meg is the complete opposite in character to Leo and Felix. She complains when she gets picked up and cuddled and will even start hissing. Then the next moment she is licking your hand apologetically. She can be a ferocious little beasty at times.

We had my Mum staying for Christmas one year and Angus, her Westie dog stayed too. He was a mature old dog and a bit blind and deaf. Meg, who was still only a kitten at the time, would sit on top of the sofa glaring down at Angus and growling under her breath. Angus was totally unaware that he was the cause of such attention and never seemed to notice her and whenever he

did catch sight of her, he would wag his little tail in a friendly sort of way and then ignore her again.

The great outdoors holds much excitement for her. Felix pops out round the block for his twenty minute stroll and is back in again but Meg is out for hours. She can be seen cruising through the bushes or chasing butterflies. Her tail appears to sweep up all the garden. It is not unusual to comb out of her fur dried leaves, twigs and the odd slug.

Animals do have their uses. One of our sons had managed to splatter his yoghurt all over the kitchen cupboards and floor.

"Right" I said, "Call in the cats!" Sure enough, the cats were very willing to help with the clearing up. Another time, down at Mum's, my sister had a similar disaster. *Splat* went the tomato soup all over the kitchen floor. Lily, my sister's miniature dachshund and Angus came to the rescue. What a delicious surprise!

Another thing about cats that is slightly annoying is that they always have a tendency to sit right in the way. The number of times we have nearly tripped over Felix as he sits in the middle of the doorway, or sits in the middle of the kitchen floor! They seem to like to be right in the middle of things. Well they are our wonderful companions after all.

Ollie The 'Orrible

Oliver was a cat with issues, serious issues. His story was told to me by a friend of mine.

He had been born on a farm and was 'partly' feral, or so the farmer who sold him to my husband one dark and cold November evening had said. Nevertheless, ignoring the warning, Clive paid the money and proudly bought Oliver home to me, his new wife.

We had been married the week before on the 31st October, Halloween, and Clive, knowing I always wanted a cat, thought it would be a fitting wedding present and so that evening, a tiny black bundle of a kitten arrived into the Leversha household.

The first thing we noticed was that he was not black, he was a very dark brown, although he had a beautiful fluffy tail that Clive would often say in the future, "Would make a lovely pair of gloves". The second thing was his tremendous appetite, he just kept coming back for more and more food, it was because of this we named him Oliver, after Oliver Twist, Ollie for short. It was some time later we realised that he had worms.

Over the next few months it became apparent Ollie was going to be more of a handful than your average moggy. His obsession with eating cactus plants, the biting of ankles when you came home after leaving him, the bullying of the local cats

and his habit of jumping out on a person from nowhere and then scratching them to pieces, limited the number of visitors that came to our home. In the summer, he decided that he rather liked a barbeque and so he would trundle off to visit which ever neighbour was hosting one that day. Of course, his temperament meant he was not the most popular of guests, but he always managed to get food, one way or another.

The months rolled on and so did the complaints from the neighbours, postman and delivery men until one evening, when Ollie had been particularly vicious and drawn blood while attacking my very patient husband, Clive snapped and decided that it was time to give Ollie a 'human to cat talking to'. This involved Clive, sporting a pair of thick leather biker's gloves, lying flat out on his stomach on the floor, pushing Ollie by the scruff of his neck down onto the floor with his face facing him, nose to nose. You would not believe the howling, hissing and attempts at scratching that came from that cat and all the time Clive would be, in his gentle voice, reprimanding Ollie on his behaviour. Clive would gently tap Ollie on the nose as he said things like, "You are a very naughty boy! You must not scratch people, you must learn to behave yourself!" This happened quite frequently but it made no difference to the way Ollie carried on. However, it always made Clive feel better.

Many times friends and relatives would, subtly at first, and then more forcefully as time went on, suggest that Ollie should be found a new home or even dispatched to the great cattery in the sky. The thing was that Clive and I had become very fond of our not so little (almost) black monster.

We loved the way he would come up on the bed in the morning and using one very sharp claw pull on one of our bottom lips to wake us up, his way of lulling you into a false sense of security by jumping on your lap, purring and then suddenly for no reason start hissing and scratching you just as you went to stroke him. Therefore when I found out I was pregnant, contrary to the advice from friends and family we decided Ollie was going to stay.

Our son arrived in the September. Ollie seemed intrigued at first and then much to everyone's amazement, it soon became clear he was not going to hurt the baby. He would just watch him and run away when he cried. I am sure if he had known the things that our son was going to put him through in the following seven years this would not have been the case.

One afternoon within a few weeks of our son's birth, Ollie came in through his cat flap crying. He had, I later found out, jumped into our neighbour's garage through a broken window that had a jagged piece of glass still in place. This

had ripped the skin from the front of Ollie's back legs right down to the bone. I was beside myself. Clive took control of the situation. He promptly took Ollie to the vets, who suggested it would be best to put him out of his misery. Clive was not convinced.

It was some hours later before Clive arrived home with a very subdued cat, who was covered in blood, the bandages that covered both his back legs beginning to show signs of continuing bleeding.

"The next 24 hours are critical," Clive said as we got the dirt box prepared should Ollie be in any fit state to use it. Both of us slept in the lounge that night monitoring the new born upstairs in his cot and this poor creature fighting for survival downstairs.

The next morning, Ollie suddenly came to as the pain relief had worn off. He was desperate to get to his dirt box and literally rolled his way to it. We had to administer tablets to him several times during that day which was not an easy task, but luckily the biker's gloves were at hand. The vet had told Clive that Ollie's bandages would have to be changed every two to three days. This would cost £150 a time (a lot on money in 1984) if done in the surgery. We had no idea where we were going to get the funds from. It was then that we hit upon the idea of changing the bandages ourselves. How difficult could it be?

A few days later, Clive and his mum, Kath, armed with a tranquiliser tablet, antiseptic cream, towels, bandages and of course the trusted biker's gloves, attempted to change Ollie's dressings. That cat may have been two legs down, but, tranquiliser or no tranquiliser, that cat could scratch for England. Although the job got done, there was still a large amount of blood spilt and it was not Ollie's.

This ordeal went on for a few weeks. One day Ollie decided he wanted to go outside, but of course he still had bandages on. The vet said it was too early but there was no arguing with Ollie. He would not be happy until he got outside, either via his cat flap or some other way. How do you prevent the back legs of a cat getting wet when covered in bandages?

"Got it!" said Clive after much thought, and off he went to the local chemist.

Some days later, Joyce the old lady who lived next door, who whenever she came to visit would drink us out of whisky, started chatting to Clive and I over the adjoining wall of our back gardens. The subject got around to Ollie, and Joyce commented that she thought he must be getting better as she had witnessed him bullying Charlie, the other neighbour's cat that morning.

"The only thing is my dears," she said. "I see you have put something over his bandages to keep them dry, but what is it?"

I looked at Clive to respond for after all it was his idea. How was he ever going to explain to her that the items covering each of Ollie's, now healing bandaged legs, were a form of contraception.

Well I thought, *at least they're black!*

Ollie the 'Orrible was written by Jane Leversha-Morris

Scampering in the Attic

I was sent to a boarding school in Worcestershire. It was not a happy experience but a couple of memories I do not mind recalling. I do remember the attics where the music rooms were located. On a summer's afternoon, it was not unusual to hear violin, piano and trumpet music echoing and floating down into the school courtyard in the centre of the school. There was a harp in one of the strange shaped tiny rooms and I did sneak in and have a quick twang.

Our school used to be an old hotel and was decorated with strange little turrets, *Continental Gothic* was the style apparently. There was also a secret tunnel from the school building to the railway station next door. Not so secret as we all knew about it but it was, of course, out of bounds. It was located at the bottom of the main staircase. At the very top of this staircase was a tiny staircase that wound its way up to a locked door. This led into the upper attics. In the sixth form, we slept under these rooms. Nobody was allowed up there.

One night I remember being woken at 6am to a thunderous noise of rodent feet scampering over the ceiling accompanied by loud excited squeaking. This happened on several occasions.

There must have been an army of rats up there. This leads on to the next story.

A Leap Too Far?

Back in our house in Somerset, we woke up one morning to noises above our heads. They were loud scratching, scampering type noises above the ceiling. Thought, *those birds are mighty loud.* In the past, we had had experience of birds clearing out our guttering looking for grubs. We would wake up in the morning to find splodges of moss splattered all over the patio. Well that is one way to clear our gutters! But that was not it.

A few weeks later all was revealed.

I was just getting into the car when my attention was attracted by a strange *guttural* sort of noise coming from the drain pipe near the garage door. When I got closer I saw there was a grey foot and what looked like a squirrel's tail sticking out of the gap at the bottom of the drain pipe. I tried to shift the pipe but could not move it on my own. One of my sons was just up the road with his teenage mates so I called them over and together we managed to shift the pipe. What was revealed was not just one baby squirrel but three! They had been living in our roof space and fallen down the drain pipe. We did not know quite what to do, so rang the local vets. They took the baby squirrels but unfortunately the one at the bottom did not survive. Who knows what happened to the rest. Perhaps they released them into the wild to scratch and scamper again?

Another time I opened the front door and suddenly, crash, a huge chunk of bread landed at my feet! Manna from heaven? No, just a passing bird dropping its titbit. At the same time, I heard a tremendous scuffling noise coming from my right. When I looked across there was a baby squirrel hanging by its paws from the guttering. Its tail was flapping furiously this way and that as it fought to find its balance. It managed to scramble back up and race across the roof. This was probably the same squirrel that found itself in the garage. We could not get it out because when cornered they can get very nasty and so there it lived for two days until it finally managed to escape.

One day things took a different turn. Chester, our cat, was acting a bit strange as if he had seen something just outside his cat flap. I looked out the back door and that is when I saw it. On the patio, a squirrel, flat on its back, legs in the air, eyes tightly shut, and definitely dead! Could this be our visitor from the attic? How did it get there? Had it leapt off the roof to the blossom tree and missed? Had Chester or Nibbles (or Nipples as my dear husband would like to call him) the

ferocious white cat from next door confronted it and won? My husband's comment was:

"Ah, my voodoo effigy of a squirrel and sticking pins into it has worked!"

It's a mystery and I guess we will never know!

All the noises from above suddenly stopped and quietness descended. The next year scratching and gnawing type noises returned to the roof space. Our lodgers are back and alive and crunching!

Oh dear!

Doggy Stories

Meg the Bull Terrier

My grandparents owned a nursery down in Kent and they had kept Bull Terriers and bred from them. As a child, I remember the long row of dog kennels at the back of the house. They looked like giant cages to me but then I was only five. My Mum and aunt carried on the family tradition of keeping these very faithful and loyal dogs.

Mum and Dad had a Bull Terrier called Meg and she had a beautiful litter of puppies. They kept

one of the puppies and named her Jenny and Jenny was the first dog that I remember.

Unfortunately Meg had a bit of a problem and my Dad made up a poem about it.
This is how it goes:

> Hold your nose, Hold your nose,
> Meg has made a smell.
> Hold your nose, Hold your nose,
> Hark she blows!

Go Home Patch!

Patch was a Greyhound/Bull Terrier cross and was Grandma's and Grandpa's first dog. When my aunt was a girl he used to escort her to the bus stop when she went to school and meet her off the bus when she came home. In the morning at the bus stop she would say to Patch,

"Go home, Patch."

and he would but what the family did not realise that for years he had taken a slight detour via the Small Boxes Grocery Store. There, they would give him a bacon bone. This he would eat before he got home.

One day, Grandma decided to escort her daughter to the bus stop and as usual, Patch came too. When Grandma called in at the shop on the way back, Patch came in too.

"You're not allowed in here," she said.

But the shop owner called out,

"Is that your dog? He's been coming in here every day for his bones!"

So Patch was busted but I guess he continued getting his bacon bones!

Another time, my uncle used to go out boxing. He climbed up into the boxing ring and the next thing they knew was that Patch was in the ring too!

"Go home Patch!"

Lily's Visit

My sister came to stay with us for Christmas one year along with her very old, black, miniature dachshund. Lily is a sweet little thing and fits very nicely into a large bag. My sister used to go and visit her son and took the train. Lily in her bag was quite the topic of conversation.

As our house is a cat zone, we were slightly nervous about the visit. As it turned out, everything ran fairly smoothly apart from a few confrontations. On Lily's arrival, the cats freaked and shot out the cat flap at a hundred miles per

hour and did not return for forty-five minutes! Even then, they lurked on the patio and did not venture in until teatime.

Lily is the most unassuming quiet little thing and did not bark. Most of the time all one could see of her was a small head peeping out of a rather large bag. She simply gazed out of her bag and quietly watched. When on the ground, the clatter of her claws on our wooden floor could, understandably be slightly alarming but otherwise, she slept. Meg was not too put out and would do her usual slink around the edges of the kitchen, check that the coast was clear through the hall and make a sudden dash for the stairs and the safety of the upstairs. Felix, the indoor cat, was a little more put out. The trouble was he kept forgetting Lily was there. He would saunter into the lounge in his usual sort of way.

Suddenly, he would catch sight of the doggy visitor, freak, and in a split second race out. All we would hear was the bang of the cat flap as he shot out to safety. Twenty minutes later, the whole drama would be repeated. He is such a wuss! After a few more days, the animals would have sorted themselves out but as it was, things were not too dramatic and the cats did not leave home.

The Star Shaped Biscuit

Roly is a Dachshund/Jack Russell cross and belongs to my sister. He has a glossy coat, a long sleek brown back and has been described as a *high energy dog*. He always greets you with an ecstatic welcome as if he had not seen you for months and his anxious brown eyes look up appealing at you. He is a very bright, loveable dog. He rushes around and as soon as you sit down he then throws himself upon your lap for a quick hug. The only problem is that he has issues,

lots of them. His biggest issue is a separation one and does not like been left too long on his own and throws back his head and howls and leaves his scratch marks on the door. His squirty collar did seem to help with his problem because when he barked he got a nasty squirt of cold water in the face. Despite his issues he is a very sweet little dog.

When I go to visit, I usually take him out for a walk and so we have developed a working relationship. He loves his walks and like everything else attacks it with his usual enthusiasm and high energy. We set off at speed down the country lane and as soon as he is let off the lead in the fields, he bounds off with great delight. He keeps on looking behind and checking to make sure he keeps in step with me. His tolerance of other dogs leaves a lot to be desired but as we have never met anyone else on our romps across the fields I have never experienced that side of his personality.

One day I was over as usual when he had just been given his breakfast. I was sitting at the far end of the kitchen at the time. Roly came over to me and very deliberately dropped a star shaped dog biscuit at my feet. It was like he was saying, "You're my friend and I want to share my breakfast with you." He gave me a little lick and went off and finished his breakfast. What a lovely gesture! I felt quite honoured. It spoke volumes about the relationship between humans and dogs.

Needless to say I did not take up his offer to eat the biscuit but appreciated the doggy thought! He is fairly settled now, and his anxiety issues? Well he still has them but he is a slightly calmer dog these days – slightly.

Funny moments with the Neighbours

We live in a quiet Somerset village, but nothing could be further from the truth. We have two cockerels nearby, one lives at the front and one at the back. One of them is definitely of a foreign variety because when it crows it sounds like it is been strangled. There are numerous birds that visit the garden, long tailed tits, sparrows, blackbirds, nuthatches, blue tits and robins. We had a tree creeper once but unfortunately one of our cats got that. There is also a ferocious wren that lives in the front. The woodpecker is pretty noisy too when it visits as it sort of cackles. It swoops down on our little tree at the front and hunts for grubs.

At night we hear the owls hooting. We do not see the badgers as they rush through our garden at night but we know they have visited because they dig little holes in the lawn and one year they dug up the carrots. The only thing that stops them passing through is a barricade of concrete slabs and bricks. Slow worms too pass through. Our cat got one once but did not know quite what to do with it.

As for human neighbours, things are not always quiet there either. I think James next door is having a stressful moment. He has three daughters – enough said. As I sit in our peaceful conservatory on a cool summer's evening, all I can hear is:

"Get in the bath!"

And again,

"Get in the bath!"

I think he must be talking to Chloe, their youngest. I first met James, who holds a very senior position in the police force, looking for their pet rabbits under one of our cars. Another time I met him, he was trying to catch a wayward chicken.

On the other side of us we have the *grumpy neighbour*. He hardly ever smiles and usually complains about most things. However, his wife is really nice. We discovered that he is very funny about his borders. He has fallen out with the

people at the back of his garden and the cause was a dispute about tree height. Meanwhile I had cut my trees on our shared border but he did not like what I had done to *my trees*. The next thing I noticed, he was adding another layer of bricks to the wall between us. I had visions of it being six feet high! As one of my sons remarked, they were surprised he did not mount gun placements on top of his walls!

Then there was the incident of the poles. While having our extension built, we had lots of workmen coming and going. Unfortunately, our plumber could not reverse up the drive in a straight line and he made a bit of a mess of the neighbour's lawn. The next day, there appeared a sort of handmade metal contraption consisting of metal poles edging the neighbour's lawn. It was extremely ugly and I had a clear view of it from our kitchen window. I was desperate to rip it out but it was suggested that I did not antagonise the neighbours.

So for two years we were stuck with the metal poles until we decided to concrete the flower border at the top of the drive. On the morning that the work was to be carried out I, with great glee, went and removed the eyesore. Within twenty minutes the neighbour was out and demanding what I was doing to his poles. I calmly explained what we were about and if he wanted to put them back in his lawn, that was fine by us but he was not to stick them in our flower border. He went off in a huff but we never saw the poles again!

Then there's Laser Man

Another neighbour we have goes by the unusual nickname of *Laser Man* or as my son calls him *Angry Man*. We gave him these names because of an incident that happened some time ago. Our middle son had his bedroom at the front of the house and one evening he had a friend over. They were messing around with a laser pen and shining it out of the window. They then noticed a man at the top of the drive looking around and trying to see where the light was coming from. He eventually tracked it down to our house.

We knew nothing of this until there was a ring on the doorbell. I was confronted with a man I did not know angrily demanding who was responsible for the shining light and demanding to speak to them at once. He was very rude and I told him quietly to wait while I went to find out. I decided to get my husband to speak to him. He was still extremely rude and started swearing so my husband calmly told him to leave. We found out later that Laser Man had been giving a dinner party when he had noticed a red light darting around his wall and had thought it was a marksman out to get them. He had insisted that his guests hide under the table. I do not know what line of business he was in or what his story was but we did not forget the incident. We found out later that he worked at the local gun shop so perhaps that explains his heightened concern. Our son's friend was told to get rid of the laser pen.

This same neighbour took our son's bike away and it took us several days to get it back. The neighbour had claimed that he had had trouble with kids before and he had chased our son's friend all the way home. As it happened, our son was completely innocent but his bike was on his friend's drive, so Laser Man took it! We went round to retrieve it and his wife, a very apologetic lady, said he had locked it in his van and driven away! A few days later a very embarrassed young constable came round and brought back the bike. She indicated that this particular man was well known to them and had often caused trouble in the past. We had no dealings with him for many years until one hot afternoon in June.

There was a ring on the doorbell and there was Laser Man.

"Can I come into your garden to catch my rooster?"

"Of course!" we said. So we left him to it, rushing up and down the lawn trying to catch his bird. The rooster was having none of it.

You're not going to catch me! and with its head darting from side to side it shot off in another direction.

A little while later I wandered round the front to see how he was getting on. I noticed he was now brandishing a large fishing net.

"Having fun?" I enquired cheerily. He gave me an exasperated look.

"He shouldn't have got out. His wings are clipped," he muttered and with that he shot off at speed down the lawn accompanied by loud clucking noises coming from under the hedge. I did not offer to help as it was too hot and chickens and roosters are notoriously difficult to catch as I had learnt on previous occasions with other neighbours.

While we are on the subject of neighbours I would like to share a statement. Young children often come out with comments that have no relevance whatsoever to the topic under discussion. Serving at Children's Church, we were working on learning the Memory Verse which was Love Your Neighbour. We were discussing neighbours when one little chap who was only four, pipes up.

"I went camping in Cornwall."

Leader, "Well yes, that's nice. You have neighbours when you're camping."

Living with Teenagers

Meanwhile back on the home front be prepared for a roller coaster of a ride when there are teenagers in the house. Life is never dull and is full of surprises. Just when you think they have discovered maturity and good sense, they will suddenly turn round and prove you wrong. We have three sons which makes life very interesting. Let me give an example, a typical day or night.

4am three year old wakes up and clambers into parents' bed and proceeds to take up all the room. 6.30am alarm goes off in teenager's room. Dad goes to investigate.

"Has your alarm gone off for any useful purpose?"

Teenager, "Don't know, can't remember." Perhaps the reply was just a grunt that came from under the bedclothes?

Another time, Dad enters teenager's room.

"Cor! It's freezing in here!" Come rain or shine, the window is always left wide open.

Another thing we noticed was that they are always eating. They come home from school and the first task is raid the fridge or raid the cupboard. A light snack consists of eight to ten buttered crackers spread with tuna and grated cheese piled up on top. Yum!

Babysitting little brother consists of romping on settee and having a yelling match and taking his toys away. But guess what? The little one loves it and takes it all in his stride. Not only does he menace little brother but he menaces the family pet – the cat. Poor cat – he gets chased out of his cat flap by little 'un and forced into loving embraces by the rest of the family pack.

Well that is life, constantly on your toes, never knowing when the next verbal attack (or sudden loving hug) will come from. Mind you, the *hug* consists of drooping round parent and sort of leaning.

Our eldest son is growing. We see eyeball to eyeball. Slowly, ever so slowly, he is overtaking me.

Homework! Well talk about living on the edge.

"When's it got to be in?"

"Tomorrow."

"Well go and do it."

Half an hour later.

"Have you done that homework?"

"No."

Exasperated parent storms off. Following morning at 6.30am homework is completed.

Then there is the sleep in. It is a miracle if the teenage son gets up before 2pm. Our son discovered the sleep in through a friend when he stayed overnight at his place. This particular friend is the master of the lie in. It made such an impression on our son that he never got up before mid-day after that visit. Of course school days are a huge effort.

As we have three sons, not only has Mum the cooking, housework and general chores to do but she must put on her referee hat as well. This means she must roll up her sleeves and intervene between physical fighting. It starts as soon as they walk through the door after school. The best solution is to sit them in front of the telly or feed them. Housework has already been mentioned and I love my youngest son's definition of housework, "Mum does random things around the house."

Living with teenagers can be summed up in a number of words.

Modesty – none.

Washing – never except under duress by insistent parent.

Pride – massive. It's the *I'm always right* syndrome.

When the going gets tough, my message to any parent out there is:
You are not alone.

One has to look on the hilarious side to keep sane. Ah! Those were the days!

Other Pets

Some people keep rabbits and some people may keep guinea pigs. We kept Russian hamsters and later rats. The Russian hamsters were horrible little creatures and *boy*! Do they bite! They also did not live very long. After the first one died within a few months, our son's friend, who was breeding them, sold us another one and gave one

for free. Buy one, get one free was the offer. This seemed like a good idea at the time. They did not last very long either so we gave up on those. Then we got two rats. They were beautiful creatures, whiskery and friendly and were very affectionate. They would perch on your shoulder and whiffle into your ear. The first pair were called Flash and the other would have been called *Ahhhh* as in Flash Gordon but that would not have worked as a name so we settled for Frisk.

The next pair were Scampers and Rascal. Rascal was a rascal too. She could undo the cage door so we had to put a padlock on it. Our son would put a rat on each shoulder and carry them round the house. From behind all you could see were two ratty tails entwined down his back.

Rats make lovely pets but they do not live long enough and two or three years seems to be their normal life span and they also have an alarming tendency to grow lumps. This means a vet job on a fairly regular basis. So, after Rascal and Scampers we decided not to have any more despite their wonderful company.

Serious Pig Incident

I cannot leave the neighbourhood stories without mentioning pigs. I wish more pig stories could be included but I have only one.

I have a special affection for pigs. Maybe it is their appealing floppy ears or their silly grunts and squeaks or maybe it is just because my dad had a fondness for them so I do too.

This story begins with the wonderful footpaths we have all around the village. They snake through the woods, twist and turn to keep pace with the hidden streams and follow the curves of the old forgotten canal routes.

Following the contours of gentle hills these paths have probably been walked for centuries. My great grandfather used to walk between his village and the next to court his sweetheart cousin, my great grandmother. That was down in Kent but life was probably not so different here in Somerset.

A group of walkers who were mature in age and were not in the peak condition that they had enjoyed in their youth, were walking their usual route at the bottom of the village. Joyce and Jim had had hip replacements a while back, Sharon had a dodgy knee, Alex was a bit asthmatic and Stan was, "Doing alright, but mustn't grumble," and always brought up the rear. They were armed with sticks and umbrellas as the weather had looked a bit uncertain when they'd started out. Menacing black clouds had clustered on the horizon and the possibility of rain was never far from their thoughts.

They had battled through the thick undergrowth in the wood below the village, avoiding tree roots, clumps of earth and small stones and now emerged into the open space at the bottom of a large field. It sloped gently up towards the first line of houses. Usually some pigs were kept here and the footpath went straight across the field. Most of the time, everything was fine, the pigs kept to themselves, happy in their muddy piggy surroundings, and walkers passed through unmolested. The field was occupied as usual. However, only one lone pig was in residence. This in itself was unusual. It looked up and surveyed the walkers with suspicion. The walkers huddled together and discussed possibilities. A plan of action needed to be decided.

"We could avoid the field and go back by the road," suggested Alex.

"It's only a pig!" said Sharon.

"Looks harmless enough," said Stan hopefully.

"I think we should risk it," suggested Jim.

So plan decided they headed up the field. What they did not know was that a pig alone is not a happy one. As they toiled up the slope, Joyce got slightly separated from the rest of the group. It was her that the pig paid attention to. Without warning and with a sinister grunt, it charged across the field. Startled, she looked in horror at the approaching animal, and hobbled to the only shelter there was, a large fence. With her back to the fence, she faced the pig that now had her pinned up against the fence. Fortunately she had her umbrella with her and using this she managed to keep the beast at bay.

"Help!" she managed to cry out, breathing heavily from her exertions with the umbrella. The pig lunged again.

"It's bitten the end of my umbrella!"

It took a while for her elderly friends to get across and rescue her from what could have been a very nasty situation. Quick as a flash Stan took off his anorak and threw it over the pig's head. Calm was restored as they made their getaway. From that moment on, Stan's nickname was to be *Pigador* for he had saved the day and his heroic deed was the talk of the local pubs for weeks on end.

When the pig owner was finally tracked down, he was very surprised that such a thing could have happened. Apparently it was the fact that the pig was on its own that had caused it to act in such a strange way. It was quickly removed and there were no lasting repercussions from the incident. So the countryside is not as quiet as it seems and care must be taken even on a gentle country stroll!

Going Slightly Quackers

I had always wanted to have my own horse and finally achieved this when I bought my faithful Misty. She was a beautiful black cob with wonderful feathery white feet. She was lovely natured and quiet to ride. She was kept at a local farm along with other horses and various animals. There was Tilly the sheep who was always getting in the way, numerous ducks who seemed to spend most of their time on the compost heap and at one time we had a stray cow and her calf living in our field. The cow was called 'Chase Her' because they could not catch her and she got in with the bull and the result was the calf called 'Tuesday'. Misty was very interested in the calf and wanted to rush over and sniff her.

The trouble with the cow was that she did not respect any of the electric fences set up in neat rows and lines to keep each horse in its own bit of paddock. We would come up in the afternoon and find that Chase Her and Tuesday had yet again crashed through all the fencing and caused a right mess. Fortunately they only lived in our field for a few months.

I went up one morning and there was no-one around. I carried on with the usual chores which involved filling up buckets with water. Suddenly, animals came from all directions, big ducks, white ducks, wild ducks and Tilly the sheep came bounding over. A torrent of quacking ensued. Must have been feeding time and the sight of the buckets had set them all off.

Keeping Misty at the farm made one very aware of the rhythms of the seasons. In the spring, the swifts would return to their nests under the eaves. If you looked up you would see a row of little heads looking down on you. The parents would swoop and dive over your head through the summer and when autumn came, suddenly, they were gone, until the next year. A woodpecker would come back every spring and lived high up in a tall tree on the edge of one of the fields. You always knew when it had returned because you would hear its loud cackle echoing in the air.

One day while doing the stable I looked up and there on the stable door was a robin. They nested in a niche in the wall just by the tack room. One beautiful May evening I went up to check the horses. Misty shared her field with Trigger, a palomino pony. Like Misty he was good natured and quiet. Trigger was looking glorious as his golden coat shone in the late warm sun and behind him I caught sight of the moon, huge and shining, hanging over the field like a large silver coin. It was lovely up there in the summer. You could imagine that you were standing on the open savannah or prairie and sense the peace and stillness. Another time I was busy 'poo picking' when I saw Misty start. I looked up and saw that Tilly the sheep had skipped up into the field. I witnessed a magic moment when she and Misty touched noses and then quietly ignored each other.

As the days shortened I would get the horses in at the edge of darkness. One time I was a bit late getting them in. It was pitch dark and I could not see them as they must have been at the bottom of the field. I stood at the top and called into the

darkness. Suddenly there was a thunder of hooves and they came galloping up the field. It was a wonderful moment.

Another time I got her in on a particularly cold afternoon in the winter and she had icicles in her mane and tail! She was perfectly alright as she had her thick winter rug on. You could see her breath hanging in clouds in the sharp cold air. I would lead her into the stable and get her ready for the night. Undoing the rug clips was particularly hard in the winter when your hands were frozen by the coldness. It was then you could feel the warmth of Misty's body as you stood beside her. When I picked Misty's feet out I would lean on her and she would lean back. Sometimes she sighed. I would hang up her hay net and loved the sweet smell of their food and hearing their contented munching as they nibbled at their hay.

Riding out in the fields was beautiful and often fairly quiet. Sometimes there were glimpses of deer. They would just be standing there in the middle of the fields. Deer are free spirits, they go where they please. Ellusive and silent they are glimpsed in a moment and then gone bounding and jumping through the crops.

Having a horse can have its funny moments. One time I had just ridden out from the farm when a car came alongside and the driver wound down the window. "Excuse me for asking," he said, "and I know this probably isn't the right word, but what species is she?"

"She's a cob. You can tell by the feathers on her feet." I said.

When I told my family about the conversation, one of my sons said, "You should have told him she was a mammal!"

Misty also shared her field with a horse called Jimmy. The trouble was Jimmy had a big problem, he was always breaking wind. Some horses do it now and then yet my Misty hardly ever did it but Jimmy was dreadful. Even the vets

thought it was quite amusing. I would be up there quietly poo picking on a summer's evening and be serenaded by Jimmy farting yet again. He must have been an embarrassment to ride! Well it takes all sorts. There certainly were some characters at the farm.

Looking after a horse is hard work and after five years of owning Misty I sold her back to her previous owner. It was a wonderful experience and there are many moments that I miss but now I am very glad that all those winter chores do not have to be done by me on freezing cold mornings and evenings any more.

Life with a Ninety Year Old

It is sometimes a daughter's dread that one day she will turn into someone just like her mother. The turbulent waters of a mother/daughter relationship run very deep. Mum and I used to muddle along quite nicely, probably because I got it all out of my system when I was a teenager. However, Mum used to drive my sister *bonkers*.

As I write about my Mum, I feel I am writing about my grandmother as well. They did not get on either. My Mum was described by a friend as a 'sweet woman'. Little did she know!

Mum was never known for her tact. She was quite outspoken but who can blame her when she had reached her nineties. It is the personal remarks that really floor one.

We used to take Mum out for meals at the pub which she thoroughly enjoyed. As we stood at the bar ordering drinks Mum asked,

"Have you got a Tio Pepe?" (a posh kind of sherry).

"No madam."

"Not much of a barman are you?"

We just had to grin and bear it and pretend we had not heard.

The Cat with a Mission

Mum's little dog Angus, a Westie, was getting on in years and we knew that the day would come when he would no longer be with us. He was Mum's constant companion so I was concerned about what to do about the situation. I was thinking about this one morning, when Felix strolled into our bedroom and parked himself lovingly on our bed, purring all the time and rubbing up against my hand. Then the idea came to me, we could loan Felix. A cat with a mission! Being the loveable cat that he is, he would certainly be the perfect companion. He is always around and hardly ever goes out except to take his usual walk round the block which takes him twenty minutes (I timed him once). I pondered on this and left it at that. When I went to visit Mum as usual the next week, she suddenly announced that she had a lodger.

"What do you mean?" I asked, conjuring up a fat rat or some massive spider that stalked across the lounge carpet. She did used to have one of these but Lily, my sister's little black dachshund ate it.

"Come with me and I'll show you," she said mysteriously. So we crept towards her utility room door that is usually kept shut to stop Angus squeezing himself out through the cat flap. We quietly opened the door. Nothing. She then explained that at night a black cat came in and slept by the boiler and sometimes he was there during the day as well. Occasionally he would get a bit bolder and come into the house. We later discovered that he belonged to the neighbours, two doors down, and his name was Merlin. His owners thought he was out hunting all night. Angus does not seem to mind him although he did chase him round the dining room table once. Merlin was certainly the answer to my prayer. Now I wonder if he could help with the passing of Angus? And so it was.

He turned out to be a very friendly cat and after Angus was gone, he would curl up on Mum's lap and even venture upstairs and sleep on her bed. It is funny how animals seem to know when to do the right thing and turn up at exactly the right moment.

I share some of the next instances because when you need to support elderly relatives, and things get tough, really tough, there are times when you need to get through situations with a sense of humour, smile, and see the funny side to life.

Mum wanted to live as independently as possible in her own home but at this stage of her life with her health deteriorating, she needed carers to come in. They were brilliant and very supportive. They would help with everyday tasks and provide meals for her. I happened to glance at Mum's care plan one day and had to smile.

Monday: Helped Mrs. R get washed and dressed and prepared breakfast. Removed dead mouse from hallway.

Tuesday: Helped Mrs. R with breakfast. Cleared away dead rat from utility room.

And so it went on. Merlin evidently was a great hunter and insisted on leaving his mark.

The Saga of the Toothbrush

Visiting Mum on a weekly basis there were always little chores or things to do.

"Can't find my toothbrush!" she announced.

I go upstairs and find two. No they are not the right ones. She has one for the morning and a different one for the night. I went upstairs again to find yet another toothbrush. It took several attempts to get it right.

Mum had always been a very tidy and organised person when she was younger. Perhps the reason for this was because she had trained as a Nursing Sister. Her house would be spick and span and housework chores were done on specific days and everything had its correct place. As she was gradually getting less able physically to do things for herself, we started having days of tidying up and would spend most of the day doing this and that and any other jobs that needed doing. Part of one afternoon was taken up sorting dusters.

"What do you mean?" I asked innocently when she asked me to help.

"The dusters and cloths are all muddled up. The carer used a dish cloth to wipe the kitchen floor the other day." So I gathered up all the dusters and brought them before her. She wanted three piles.

"Why?" I asked. She explained that the first pile was for glass dusting only, the second pile for silver and the third pile was dish cloths for the kitchen.

"Why different dusters for glass?"

"So that you don't get the grease on the glass."

Perfectly logical! She also had numerous chopping boards, one for meat, one for fish, one for vegetables, one for... I do not recall. It all drove my sister potty! Mum used to organise her kitchen like a military operation but that was how she was.

Eventually Mum needed a live-in carer. Under Mum's stern direction, this was accomplished but sometimes it led to friction as Mum knew her own mind. Her body was getting frailer but mentally she was fighting fit. In the media there had been reports about bad practise taking place in care homes.

"All this talk on the telly about bad care in nursing homes. Well you could have a job at ninety four." I said. "You could go in as a spy *under cover*, see what goes on and report back." Now there was a thought. That made her laugh!

Even when she had a spell in the local hospital the year before, she had managed to build up her network of supporters and allies. She was friends with someone on the night staff, someone in catering who knew what she liked and always made sure she got small portions and so the list went on. This was typical of Mum. She came out well and made a good recovery on that occasion.

Her sense of humour was never far away. Walking along the street in Street, Mum was using her hospital stick.

"Every time I see someone walking along using a similar stick, I feel we ought to salute!" she remarked.

The first live-in carer was foreign and although a nice girl, she did not hit it off with Mum. Living with Mum was always going to be a challenging opportunity. According to Mum, Lana had no sense of humour and apparently used to mutter under her breath. Mum could not hear her very well. Now whether this was due to the mumbling or due to Mum's lack of hearing, we were never quite sure but at one of the meetings with the supervisor, Mum suggested in a very loud voice,

"She needs speech therapy."

I did suggest to Mum afterwards that this remark was a bit rude! Mum stuck to her guns, outspoken as usual. Often, she was right. It just was not expressed with any tact!

The Lettuce Incident

Most of the time things ran fairly smoothly but just occasionally there were little hiccups along the way. Mum, being the age that she was, was

very much set in her ways and one of these was how she liked her little gem lettuce cut up. I asked her how she was getting on with Lana. She gave me a funny look and told me that she only got the outer leaves of her lettuce and not the succulent tasty middle heart. She had even shown Lana how to cut the lettuce in half but, yet again, at teatime, there arrived the darker green outer leaves and no heart. Eventually my sister took up the challenge and talked to the carer and things improved.

The next carer on the scene was wacky Dorita from Poland. A kind person and as big as a house but definitely a bit strange. Mealtimes would always be a bit of a surprise but Mum had to grin and bear it. Another time we found Dorita doing the dishes with a duster. I took her into Glastonbury once and she loved it.

"Oh I could live here!" she said. *Yes*, I thought to myself, *you would fit in very well here!* Then we had Welsh Mary and she was the perfect carer. What a lovely woman. She and Mum hit it off immediately. It was such a shame we did not have her in the first place.

Mum was always able to see the funny side of life even when things were becoming increasingly difficult for her and one of her favourite jokes at this time is recorded on the next page.

How to live a long life

A tough old cowboy from Texas told his grand-daughter that the secret of a long life was to sprinkle a pinch of gun-powder on her oatmeal every morning. She did this right up to the day she died at 108 years old.

She left behind 18 children, 35 grand-children, 52 great-grand-children, 29 great-great-great-children and an enormous great hole where the crematorium used to be.

I went to visit Mum the following week when half way through the conversation I noticed that she was wearing a sort of harness belt-type arrangement around her middle. I had visions of her bungee jumping off Wells cathedral or something just as dramatic.

"Ah, I was going to get round to telling you about that," she said. The Occupational Therapist had left it to help us get Mum up out of her chair. By this time, she had no strength left in her arms to push herself up. The Occupational Therapist had been fantastic. Every time there was a different physical challenge, she would come up with a solution. Mum's house was slowly filling up with equipment, both large and small and it seemed to change almost daily. Mum had always been into her gadgets. Thumbs up to the council and all the support agencies out there for they do a wonderful job.

Mum's passing was very swift at the end. She managed to stay in her own home which was what she wanted. She loved watching telly, the Antiques Road Show and the quiz shows to name but a few but it is a shame that she never got to find out who won the Strictly Come Dancing that year.

Birdie Stories

The Raven

This story comes from John and takes place in the early 1950s. John was eighteen years old and was training for the RAF. He had finished basic training and was now completing a Fitters Course at St Athans near Gileston in Wales. The billet, which was really a hut, catered for twenty eight people and they had come together from all parts of the country. "Us peasants" as John puts it, slept in the fourteen beds that lined each side of the hut and at the end of the billet were two rooms that housed the Senior COs.

Now one chap, who was a Londoner like John, owned a motorbike. He went home on leave as usual but when he came back,

"Lo and behold he brought a raven with him," says John.

The bird tapped at the window and was asking to come in! It had just turned up!

"I think the guy was as surprised as everyone else was!"

The bird, which turned out to be his pet, had followed him all the way from London.

"We thought it was quite a novelty," says John.

"What was he called?" I asked.

"Blackie."

"What did he do when you were all out and about training?"

"He just flew around or perched here and there."

"Didn't anybody else notice him?" I asked a bit puzzled.

"No, didn't seem to, but you always knew when he was in the billet because you just had to call, 'Blackie, Blackie' and there would be an answering, 'Caw, caw.'"

John adds, "It was rather unique but when you're doing training you've got other things on your mind."

They fed him anything that came to hand which was usually bread. Blackie would walk around among them and would jump up on the chap's bed. He was attached to his owner like a dog.

"We all thought it was a laugh having a bird following you around."

Training was hard and vigorous. Discipline was very strict. You had to get up, get dressed, polish the brass on the window frame, make sure your window was clean, sweep under your bed space and polish the lino. Blankets had to be folded and stacked to military standard. All of this had to be completed before breakfast. Then 'Officer Billet Inspection' took place.

"Well of course you've got a damn bird. If it hadn't gone off it stayed under the bed," exclaims John. The officer walked down the room and at some point he must have been aware of the bird under the bed but he did not say a word and completely ignored it.

"What happened to him afterwards?"

"Can't remember. I think the bloke Blackie got attached to, took him home."

When I next spoke to John about all this he remembered that the bloke did indeed take the bird home but when he returned he made sure Blackie was in his cage and he was left at home to be looked after by his parents.

Kipper Pie

Among the many duties required was something called Station Duty. This could consist of Guard Duty or working in the cook house, peeling potatoes, opening tins of baked beans and

"If you were really unlucky, you could be put on the breakfast shift." John goes on to elaborate.

"At 4am, you would be down at the cook house cutting bread and making toast. The bread was put in large pans in the top of the oven. These were big commercial ovens and the toast went hard."

He then told me that the toast would be left on top of the ovens.

As breakfast time approached an order would be shouted out.

"Right, bring out the hose!"

The toast would then be sprayed and the heat from the ovens below would warm it up.

"So this would make it soft again," explains John with a grin.

While the men were eating their meals in the cook house the Serving Officer of the day would ask,

"Any complaints?" If you did have a complaint, you would have to stand up and the Officer was required to come down and sample the food. Not many complained.

There was however one incident worth mentioning. No food was wasted in the Forces.

On one occasion there were kipper left-overs. These were put in trays, bones and all, and covered with pastry. This delightful meal was dished up for supper. The bones were all mixed up with the pastry. *Kipper Pie* did not go down very well.

John adds, "We all complained about that one." Such is life in the Forces.

They get Everywhere

This next story is a bit closer to home. I go shopping in Bath most weeks and enjoy drifting through one of the large retail stores there. On this occasion I was helping a friend choose a birthday card.

"Oh look!" she said, "There's a pigeon!"

I followed her gaze upwards to the top of the card stand and sure enough there was a pigeon perched right on the top. It was then that we noticed two shop assistants standing very still nearby and watching the bird intently. They were obviously on *Pigeon Duty*.

"He's been in before that one. We have to keep an eye on him and see where he goes," one of them said without taking their eyes off him. Well with the food market in the next aisle we were not surprised that they were taking his visit very seriously! We have seen a variety of things in this store but never livestock before.

Yvonne's Chicken Story

Every week, I go into Bath and play Bridge. We play in a Georgian room that overlooks the beautiful, elegant Queen's Square. Sometimes in the summer you can look across down through the trees and catch flashes of light as the fire conjurers practise their tricks for their street show. Bath is alive with buskers and artists and music drifts round narrow alley ways and nearly every street corner.

The room we play in is large and grand and dominated by huge paintings on the ceiling. Bridge is a sociable past-time and there are some really nice people. Yvonne is a lovely lady I know. She told me a story about her chickens.

She has three lovely ladies called Henny, Penny and Jenny. Henny has shiny black feathers and is noisy and bossy. Penny is dark brown and speckled and keeps to herself while Jenny is plain brown and is the quiet one.

One night Yvonne woke up to hear a strange noise, a sort of tapping noise. There was a bit of wind that night and she knew there was some loose guttering and thought that it was that. Again, she heard tapping but very sporadic, there seemed to be no pattern to it. Anyway, it kept happening. Then there was tapping once again and a surprised chicken noise - Cluck!

Well she thought the chickens must be out so in the morning she asked her husband to go and check on them. Both the doors on the henhouse were locked but Jenny was gone!

What had happened is this:-

On the side of the henhouse is a laying shelf with a lid. This hadn't been locked because the hens didn't use it. However, a fox had been snooping around that night and had been lifting the lid (the tapping noise) to try and get to the chickens and had finally succeeded because there were feathers everywhere and Jenny had gone!

Experiencing the Real Italy

It had been many years since I was last in Italy. My fear of flying had taken care of that, but now I was here. I stood on the upper terrace of our fabulous palace of a hotel and gazed across the bay at the misty shape of Vesuvius rising up above the cool blue waters. It was not yet 10am and the intense heat had not started yet but it promised to be another very hot day.

Breath-taking scenery surrounded me. In front, the blue sea shaped by the curve of the coast was streaked by white flecks of boats crossing the bay. Beside me, houses clung to the ragged hilltops and sloped their way down to the beautiful town of Sorrento. The bustle and noise of the road drifted up from below. Behind me was the constant drone of crickets in the olive trees and here and there were strange tall trees that seemed to end up with palm like branches clustered at their very tops.

I breathed it in.

We had decided to hire a car for the day and venture out on our own. This would be a real adventure after experiencing the guided tours on offer to Pompeii, Herculaneum and Naples. This time it would be just us and we would soon discover our limited commands of the Italian language. We were on a mission of discovery. My Mum, who had been a Queen Alexander nurse, had been stationed in Italy during WW2 and we were keen to find a few of the locations that she had been posted to. I had published her diary and we had a copy of the book with us.

The fun started when Larry went down to the town to collect the hire car. After a considerably long time, he returned with a tale to tell.

"Do you want to hear the story of the three cars?"

Puzzled we said, "Yes."

First he was presented with a two seater. No, that will not do, there are four of us. So they found a nice suitable car and Larry started filling out the paperwork. While he was doing this there was a loud crunch outside. Someone had driven into the very car that Larry was going to take out! Good thing the paperwork had not been finished. So onto car number three. This took some time as it was at the car wash. Finally it was ready, a nice little Fiat 500. We were set to go.

Have to take my hat off to Larry and his driving, he did brilliantly. Italians do not drive the same as us in England. We are bound by rules and regulations and these make us safe or so we are led to believe. In Italy, there are fewer rules and they drive by instinct.

"I drive and let it happen!" says Larry confidently. He said the little car drove like a roller skate, neat and compact. We feel conspicuous – no dents on the car.

Jill and I had elected to sit in the back. In this way if there were any heated arguments we could not be blamed.

"You watch the road and I will press the buttons," says my husband. We still had not figured what did what as we drove down the busy, windy road into Sorrento. Mopeds come at you from every direction. Even dogs are on board as well as children sitting in front of the driver holding onto the handlebars. It all seems a bit chaotic.

At last we left Sorrento behind with its beautiful coloured plates, jugs and dishes, wonderful tablecloths decorated with lemon and olive combinations or tomato themes and carried on along the peninsula towards Castellamare.

Our goal at Castellamare was to locate the palace where my Mum was stationed in December 1943 after she arrived in Naples.

We wound our way slowly up a small insignificant road, and then we came upon it. A grand gateway. Two massive red brick pillars topped with white domes flanking a long avenue of trees. Right at the very bottom of the avenue is glimpsed a white archway set in red brick. An entrance fit for a palace, a palace that once belonged to the King of Naples. In December 1943 Mum found it as a hotel but in a very rundown, neglected state.

Now as we drive up, we are amazed at its red brick and white painted majesty. As we step out of the car we are aware of the wonderful tranquillity of the place. Set half way up a mountain, the hills continue to roll up behind, their tops shrouded in mist. The windows are large and imposing and stacked three floors high. An overgrown terrace is glimpsed through iron gates and the building towers up for four or five floors.

It was at this point that a nun appeared nearby emerging from a small convent further down the hill. I rushed over to her, keen to practise my newly learnt Italian. I had not been able to use any of it in Sorrento because everyone spoke English.

"Parla Inglese?" I enquired enthusiastically. Unfortunately she only knew French and some other language so that was my one and only attempt to speak Italian during our entire holiday. Well at least I tried.

We walk up the slope to the arched entrance not quite sure what to expect. Walking through the archway we encounter a small grass area surrounded by trees and a terrace decorated with huge urns overflowing with flowers. It is here that we meet the custodian of the museum and in broken Italian, try to explain our reason for visiting. We show him the book and the photograph of my Mum in battledress uniform and the date of 1944 printed underneath. Whether he understood our mission we do not know, but he invites us in anyway. We enter in and climb up wide steps that take us to the first floor and into the museum. It is small and compact and very clean with its various rooms and white walls.

Then we walk out onto the wide spacious terrace positioned at the front of the building. There the scene stretches away and in the far distance can be seen the clear blue outline of Vesuvius. Now the palace contains a museum and a series of flats and is still under renovation.

In all my stay in Italy, visiting this building was the icing on the cake for me as we followed in Mum's footsteps.

We continued on our journey. As we approached the toll for the motorway, Larry suddenly realised he did not know how to wind down the window.

"Which button? Help!"

We stopped and he opened the door but just in time, found the right control. The ticket person did not smile or give us a funny look at our strange antics.

Coming off the motorway and back on the main roads junctions were interesting. Priorities?

"It's a question of who is bravest," exclaims Larry and adds coolly, "Just let it happen – don't panic."

We reached our other place of interest, Nocera. The place is set in a valley and everywhere you look there are steep rocky hills. We were looking for the hospital were my Mum was working in January 1944. Our goal was a hill right in the middle of the valley and right at the very top was a castle. We needed to go up there, at least that was what we thought our sat nav was telling us. Well our little car started up very bravely but it soon became apparent that it was struggling. It was also getting very hot, us and the car. We bailed out and Larry drove on up and disappeared around the next corner. At the top we seemed to be in the middle of nowhere. The intense heat and the sound of crickets buzzed all around us. Nocera sprawled at our feet and sloping wooded hillsides trailed off down to the distant sea. It was quite stunning. Feeling tired, frustrated and pretty sure this was not the spot we were looking for, it was definitely time to get some refreshment. So we bundled back into the car to go back down into town and find a café. Our little car was much happier going down and even though the corners were rather sharp we made it safely down to the bottom.

We found a car park that appeared to be made out of scaffolding and set off down the dusty street. We were getting stared at. This place was definitely off the tourist route. We eventually found a quiet café and sat outside. Our waitress did not speak English and our Italian being a bit limited we all resorted to sign language and gestures. We were delighted when she brought out a huge plate of small pieces of pizza, tiny chip sandwiches and other snacks all carefully prepared and looking delicious. It was a real feast. We drank lemonade from large jam jars and felt refreshed. The loos were interesting. Jill and I went across the road and walked through the long cool length of the empty café to discover that the ladies had no light and you had to pull a pink string to make the loo flush. Well this was Italy after all.

We set off again. After some time of searching, driving up and down the main road we had to admit defeat. Time was ticking on and so we took the roads back through all the little towns. The afternoon got hotter and the traffic seemed to intensify. Larry certainly had his wits about him. Our journey is punctuated with cheerful comments like, "I'm signalling. Spot the tourist!" cries Larry.

Suddenly my husband says, "Mind the wall!" To which Larry replies with exasperation, "I'm minding this car on the other side!" Fortunately we missed both but it was close. Cars and mopeds mingled before us, beside and behind us.

"Not using your horn enough Babe!" comments Jill from the back.

At last we reached Sorrento and managed to wind our weary way back up to the hotel, tired but fulfilled. I think Larry enjoyed himself. He really did get into the Italian zone.

My Granddad's Garden of Delights

I was introduced to gardening by my Granddad on my Mother's side. A quiet and loving man I fell under his spell at an early age and loved nothing more than helping him in the garden. Through him I learnt about the turning of the seasons and the cycles of nature. What to plant when, when to harvest, how to ensure the fertility of the soil and the interconnectedness of all of nature and our place in it.

It is through him that I discovered I had 'green fingers', which is strange considering I spent most of my time in the garden up to my elbows in mud! I once made a festive mud pie and topped it off with a sprig of Holly. I left this in the garden and paid no more thought to it. That small sprig of Holly took root and grew into a huge Holly bush which continued to thrive in the garden long after my Grandparents had left.

One of my Granddad's many sayings which he was fond of repeating was "Front for show back to grow." I now realise that this is quite a common saying but at the time through my childish eyes, I thought this was great wisdom! He meant of course that you put all your showy plants and flowers on display in the front garden, whilst all the productive plants like fruit and vegetables were grown out of sight in the back garden. He also had an allotment nearby and I don't remember my Grandmum having to buy any vegetables and rarely any fruit.

In the front garden I particularly liked the snapdragons which you could turn into a hand puppet by placing your fingers in the lobe like petals of the flower. As well as Antirrhinums there were French Marigolds, Lobelias, Gentians and Sweet Williams, which made for a colourful display. Indeed he won several council awards for his front garden displays.

I liked the Autumn best, not just because it was my birthday but because of all the wonderful things there were to harvest. One of my favourite places to hide at this time of year was in the fruit trees at bottom of the garden. There was an Apple tree, a Pear tree and a Victoria Plum tree. When I didn't want to be found these provided a refuge and a snack, Yum!

In Autumn the outhouse was like an Aladdin's cave of delights, Apples were picked wrapped in newspaper and stored in wooden trays, where they would keep over Winter. Red cabbage and shallots were stored in huge pickling jars on shelves, excess plums and raspberries were turned into jam and stored on the shelf below. Onions had been tied together and hung from the rafters in strings and just outside potatoes had been earthed up in a clamp for later use in the Winter. And what was better than preparing all these goodies, why eating them of course over the coming winter months.

One Edward Street

The first nine years of my life were spent growing up in a Georgian town house in Bath. 1 Edward Street was just off of Great Pulteney Street close to what is now the Holburne Museum. Sydney gardens, Henriette park and the then disused Kennet and Avon canal, these were my Georgian playgrounds.

The house was to me a fairy tale castle complete with dungeon, ghosts, and witches, though most definitely good witches. Miss Loads and Miss Dark were actually my parent's landladies, but to me two old ladies living together could only have been witches. However the most glorious part of the house was the beech wood banister which descended from the Attic to the Hallway in one unbroken and unencumbered spiral and which, my trousered bottom polished on many an occasion.

The massive polished black front door with its brass knocker and its huge brass door knob set in its centre was as big as any castle gate and just as heavy. Above the knocker was a large brass number one which gleamed like gold against the blackness of the door. Once inside you entered a cavernous hallway, on the left was the largest hallway stand I had ever seen. It was like a giant's throne, there was a large seat with a lift up lid, either side of which were arms with slots for umbrellas and walking sticks. Above the seat was a long vertical mirror and at its highest extent a row of bronze coloured hooks. High above this on a shelf lay a large rectangular glass case, which contained the most intriguing mechanism. It consisted of a large circular can driven by clockwork. Wrapped around the can was graph paper and small arm held a small ink nib which tracked up and down the graph paper creating a small mountain range of lines. It was of course a barometer but to me it could have been anything and in my imagination I invented many uses for it, including a, giant detector.

The first room of the house was off this hall, originally the reception room it was now where the witches lived. Here they lured me in with biscuits and sweets and held me rapt under their spell with tall tales of Alice and Dorothy and their adventures in fantastical lands.

Further along the hallway were the stairs that lead down to the dungeon and I would never venture down there without an adult. I often accompanied Miss Loads down to the kitchen below stairs to help her prepare Miss Darks supper. Especially as I got all the buttery crusts that were cut off her pieces of bread. There was a door from the servants' day room into a small courtyard garden surround by high walls. On either side were two beds of a kitchen garden on one side grew herbs and on the other salad vegetables. At the other end of the room was the back door and beyond this under the road lay the wash house complete with boiler and mangle. Next to this was the door to the dungeon, actually the coal cellar complete with coal hole, padlocked and chained to keep whatever lay beyond from breaking out.

Beyond the end of the hall lay the first flight of stairs which lead to the first floor and the landladies' bedrooms that they no longer used as they slept down stairs, within were many curiosities which made it one of my favourite rooms. Next to this bedroom was our bathroom the main resident being a large cast iron enamelled bath with four great lion paws for feet which I felt had the ability to run off with me whilst taking a bath at the slightest whim. Also residing in the bathroom was a large black table with a heavy white marble top and drawers with pendant like draw pulls. Standing on the marble top was a vast white bowel and jug waiting to catch the blood of their next victim.

Two further flights of stairs took you up to our main living area which consisted of a kitchen/diner and a living room/dining room. These I inhabited everyday so held no magic for me. The final two flights of stairs took you up to the attic where my bedroom was next door to my parents. This is where the ghosts lived though they generally left me alone they would keep me awake at night with their constant whispering until I told them to shut up, at which point all would go quiet and I could sleep again, well at least until the local screech owl would come and wake me up!

I had many adventures in and around this house far too many to tell at one sitting.

Written by Scott G Hutchinson

A Tale of Two Guinea Pigs

Here is a tale of two guinea pigs,
One ginger and one cream.
One day in July in the bright warm sun,
They were out in the run,
Having lots of fun,
When all of a sudden, something terrible
happened,
Whilst their mistress indoors was nigh.
Someone came quickly and took them away,
On that awful day,
And left us all wondering why?

The terrible crime was then reported,
By our shocked and devastated daughter.
Photos and notices – "Has anyone seen them?"
Were put through peoples' doors.
A search on the internet went out,
From the South to the far Northern moors.
Three weeks went by,
Since the end of July,
When the animals disappeared.
"Where are they now – these beautiful sows?"
Our thoughts were full of fears.

Then eight weeks passed and still no sign.
"Should this be where I draw the line?"

My daughter said, as she sat in bed.
And then, there came a chance to obtain
Another guinea pig again.
What joy for sure to have one more.
She had been pushed out of the way, every day
By four large sows where she used to live.
And she would run and hide in the hay.
My daughter said, "A home I could give,
To this sweet little sow right now!"
So it was so good that my daughter could,
Give her a home where she could roam,
In peace and be loved and cherished,
And cared for all on her own.

This one furry mound coloured ginger and black,
With a splash of white on her nose.
Moving on the ground is such a delight,
Wherever she comes and goes.
She rocks in her tunnel, such an amusing sight!
And although she has enjoyed her time on her
own,
It is good for a guinea pig to share her home.
So for a while,
A friend came to stay,
Another sweet sow,
So suddenly now,
There are two guinea pigs in the hay!
She is torty and white,
A beautiful sight.
She makes my daughter smile!

And after a while,
These sweet little guinea pigs play, eat and sleep
together
And they shall stay together, whatever!

When next Summer comes,
They will be out in the run,
Eating the grass so green.
But they will not be left out on their own,
For my daughter will be there,
Sitting on a chair,
Enjoying the beautiful scene.
It could be one day,
In a miraculous way,
The first two will return.
At the moment it's hard to tell.
But wherever they are,
And how near or far,

We pray they are safe and well.
So here this tale ends,
For the time being at least.
But it will be miraculous for sure,
If of their whereabouts we should learn,
And these stolen ones should return,
Then there will be four!

A true story written by Sally Appleby.
Dedicated to her daughters, Roseanne and Carmen.

Mission Impossible

As a group of friends we wanted to arrange a surprise get-together for Judith's birthday. We wanted to invite her son but there was a problem. Adam does not communicate through normal channels like the rest of us. He does not answer the phone, he is not on Facebook, does not appear to do email and never uses a mobile phone. The only way to communicate with him is face to face or through his mum. Since it was his mum's surprise party that was not an option. So the only way was to give our friend Simon a secret mission as he was often at their house.

This is the email from Simon.

I had a word with Adam which was frankly less productive than pouring tea from a chocolate urn! Firstly, he had no idea whether he was working but if he was he said he could get an early shift. He said there was a calendar in the kitchen which said what weekends he was working but when I checked it surreptitiously feigning interest in the recipes on the notice board, I couldn't decipher the scrawl.

So, I then resorted to subtly interrogating Sid (his dad) about whether Adam was going to Larry and Jill's with them or was he working. (The plan was to have the surprise party on the same weekend that Judith and Sid were staying with Larry and Jill.)

This all elicited a big fat zero. By this time I was losing the will to live and decided to drown myself in cider!

The upshot of all of this, I still don't know if Adam is working Saturday 30th or not and as far as I could tell nether did anyone else!

Simon

My husband's email reply read:

Well you just give up sooo easily :-)

At our next weekly get-together, we found out via general conversation that Adam was not working that particular weekend. Hopefully Judith did not suspect anything. Simon will be dining with the Smiths this Friday. We have the green light for Adam. Go Simon go!

All was accomplished and the party went very well and Judith was surprised. Mission impossible was completed!

A Magical Story

This imaginative story is set in the Radstock Museum that celebrates the Victorian way of life and especially features the coal mining that used to dominate this area of Somerset.

Among the exhibits are various stuffed animals, the sleeping cat in the cottage, the canary in the mine, a racing pigeon and two rats. There is also a display containing a beautiful dragonfly. The inspiration for the story is based around the idea that these creatures come to life at night.

And so it begins.

"Now where is that pen? I'm sure it was on the desk yesterday."

The late afternoon sun slanted through the windows of the museum. It was time to go home. Mrs. T sighed, locked up and left the museum.

Much later as dusk fell all was quiet and still. One by one the stars started to come out. All was still quiet in the museum or was it?

There was a scampering and a rustle and a little brown nose with twitchy whiskers peered round the corner of the mine. Rascal the rat was awake and lifted up her nose to sniff the air. Nobody was around and the coast was clear. Quick as a flash she scampered past the smithy, past the outside toilet and wash house with the washing dangling overhead and jumped up onto the barrier that contained the cottage.

The cat was still asleep on the old chair but Scampers, the other rat, was alert in her corner, her little brown eyes twinkling at her sister. Quickly Scampers jumped up beside Rascal and together they ran off to cause some mischief in the schoolroom.

Cat opened one eye and then the other. Something had disturbed her. Slowly she got up, arched her back and stretched the whole length of her black and white body. As she was awake she decided to do her usual patrol of the museum and see what those rats were up to.

Who would wake up next?

There was a loud buzzing sound. Cat looked up and caught a flash of blue as dragonfly flew down the corridor.

Then a cheep cheep noise came from the depths of the mine. Canary was awake. She stretched her neck and flapped her yellow wings. Time to leave her little cage and explore. She carefully opened the latch and hopped out. There was no glass window to keep her in and so off she flew into the gloomy space of the coal mine. She flew round the corner to see her friend Polly the pigeon. Polly was still in her cage. In her day she had raced across the countryside but now she preferred to sit and preen her grey feathers.

An excited squeak came from under the Dunce's hat in the schoolroom. Cat peered in. What were those rats up to? The rattle of the abacus caught Cat's attention and there was Scampers running along the top, her tail swishing to help her balance.

Everyone was awake and busy. Cat decided to go upstairs and walk past the displays. There was Nelson's ship and further along an old bugle caught her eye as it shone in the World War 2 display. She checked under the gramophone and then came back downstairs.

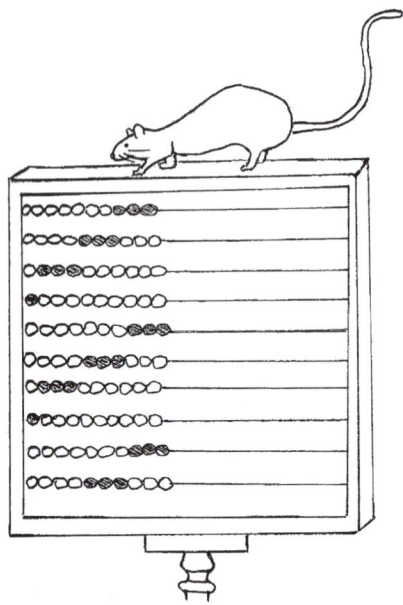

Meanwhile the rats continued to play all night, sometimes hiding in the smithy or chasing each other in the Victorian Co-op Shop. They would rush along the counter and knock the scales. Sometimes they got up onto the shelves amongst the cornflake packets and tea. They might even get as high up as the coloured biscuit tins or jump down to the shelf where the long bars of smelly soap were kept.

As dawn light crept under the shades in the book shop Rascal realised that it was time to return to the mine. She nudged Scampers to remind her to return to the cottage. Day was nearly here and the magic of the museum would soon fade away. Cat came back to the cottage and sat before the large black range. Soon, she jumped up onto the chair and curled up to go back to sleep again.

The key turned in the lock and Mrs. T came in and started her day in the book shop. Before she started work she checked round each room and display.

"Now that's strange, the Dunce's hat wasn't on the desk before or was it?"

She returned it to the shelf where it normally stood.

Another day had begun and soon the visitors would flock in. The animals are still now but if you look carefully at Scampers you may catch a twinkle in her small brown eye and if you listen you may just hear a quiet snoring as Cat sleeps on the kitchen chair by the fire.

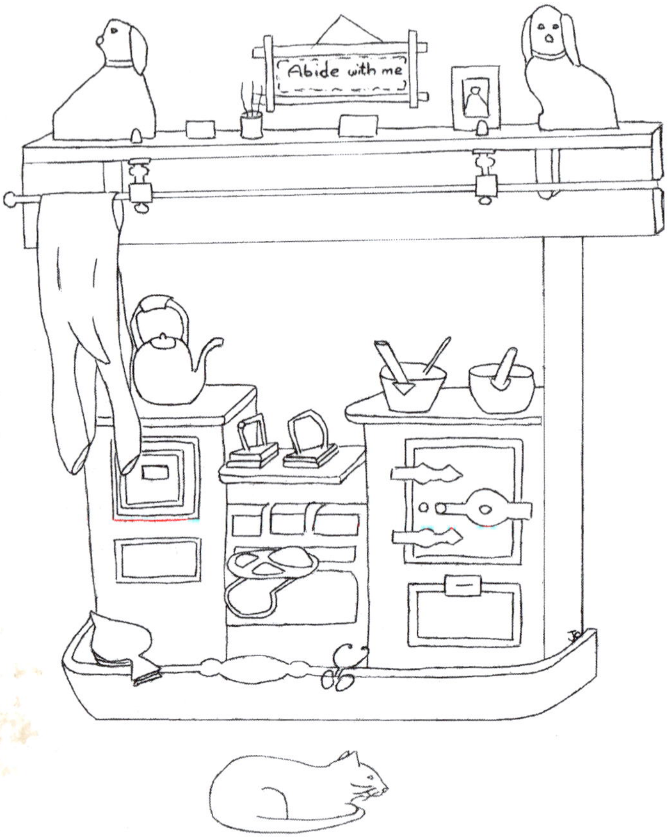

Abide with me

Drifting on the Canal

This next piece of writing is a little bit different from the previous stories. When I was a student back in the 1970s a group of us decided to take a holiday on the canal and I wrote about my impressions of this experience.

We arrived at Brauston Marina to claim our seventy foot long narrow boat monster. She was not particularly glamorous as she was a retired coal boat and still had her green canvas covering her from end to end. Inside was very basic but adequate and we were not fussy. We were given a very long pole in case we got stuck in the bank and after a brief lesson on control and steering we were off. They cheerily waved us goodbye and told us they would see us in two weeks time.

The Day of Beginnings

To drift on the canal in a narrow boat is like stepping into another world. It is like gliding through a dream, like a drop of stillness from eternity. Gone is the surge of human bustle crowded with cars, trains and busy streets. Here, there is no discord. Here, there is only simple peace and a tranquillity that seeps into one's very heart. The spell is all around you, beside you and within you on the silent waters of the canal. The boat glides on.

Pairs of Swans swim on their way under the drooping trees, bowing and swaying to each other with their long white necks bending like question marks. Nearby clusters of energetic ducks zoom in a flurry after the boat attentive for bread. Little bright eyes twinkle from brown tufts of feathers. From yellow beaks they produce loud quacking noises punctuated by splashing water as all dive for the pieces of their expectation. Moorhens dabble in the shallows and scatter across the fields.

And here, by the weeds and boat, a brown waterrat is seen travelling from hole to hole or riding the wake of the boat to visit his cousin across the water. He is just a little fellow with whiskers and tiny feet but he knows precisely what he is about and where he is going. Sometimes one will vanish into the reeds and then reappear to wash his furry tummy with his quick nimble feet.

And then there are the cows. They line the field edges like silent crowds and munch contentedly while gazing placidly into sky and bushes. They show no fear of interruption in their meditative thought as the narrow boat chugs by.

One can be woken by the cock crow. Imagine the cock standing on tip-toe, stretching his neck, vibrating his wings and uttering a cry as loud and as startling as his little body is able. Then, from another direction there is an answering crow. with enthusiasm the first crows again. Suddenly the whole valley is ringing with cockerels answering and calling to each other over and over again. Like stereo the cry is slung backwards and forwards through the frosted air, now louder, now softer.

Then as suddenly as it began, it ceases.

Not only can one be woken by cockerels but by people as well. One morning we had the saga of Mrs. Collins and partner. A man walks along the plank at the top of our boat.

Mrs. Collins "Get off that boat. That's not your boat."

Man "It's nothing to do with you."

Mrs. C "That boat is outside my pub and I'm responsible for it."

Then,

Mrs. C again. "What are those workmen doing?" There is a distant noise of drilling.

Man "Just cement mixing."

Mrs. C "They're too noisy."

Man, sounding slightly irritated, "They haven't made a speck of noise."

Mrs. C "Oh yes they have, every day for weeks now. I'm beginning to lose my custom because of them." She goes on complaining at length.

Man "You get angry far too easily Mrs. Collins."

Mrs. C "You said they would have finished ages ago and yet they're still here. I've a good mind to move them myself."

Man "Your attitude is all wrong."

Mrs. C goes on and on about the workmen until,

Man, interrupting, "Oh you do get me angry Mrs. Collins."

Mrs. C "You're just stupid."

Man "Careful."

Mrs. C "What did you say?"

Man "You heard."

Living on a boat on the canal can also have its hazardous moments. Trudging out to the pub for instance sounds simple enough, but on a cold miserable wet night, the expedition can turn into a nightmare. The boat is tied up by a soggy verge of muddy grass and the puddle strewn path wanders off into the gloom. It is a foul night. It is even worse coming back after a few drinks.

The Day of Contrast

What is so fascinating is the different scenery one passes through. Sometimes the land is level, sometimes the canal lies above it and brief glimpses of fields are seen through branches of trees on a lower level. Memories of the wide roads of southern France that run through flat countryside are conjured up along with their monotonous rows of trees that line each side like pillars.

Sometimes one passes through a small village. The back gardens, crammed with vegetables, flowers and old wooden fences. They slant down to the water's edge and tickle the verges of the old canal.

Then there are the banks piled high with hedge and thick bush. These bushes drape down to the waterside and line it in tranquillity. Sound is muffled in their trailing arms. Maybe on the other side there is a small dark wood. Peering into this wood, one can see trees standing haphazardly and silent. Roots lie naked on nut brown soil and the sky is obliterated by a generous leaf roof making the wood appear dusky and sinister.

But the most striking scenes of all are the contrasts between country and town. The country, whether woody, bushy or simply made up of fields, is always peaceful and still. Always the water leading the way, sometimes curving and sometimes straight. But the town it is a different matter. The water winds on as before but now back gardens appear and huddle closely in the shadows of houses. Perhaps a road runs parallel and is later scooped up among the buildings. Dirty looking bridges are passed under and musty walls begin to loom up on each side. The canal meanders lazily further into the midst of urbanisation, whose presence is heralded by rubbish fringing the water edges. Another bridge comes into view. The main road it carries is lined with shops and people. Cars zoom by in an endless rush and the people stagger hither and thither loaded with parcels and bags. The noise and the bustle sounds alien and strange to one sitting on the old barge just before the bridge. But the boat passes swiftly down through the locks and glides under the bridge like a phantom from another era, left over from a time past.

Suddenly the deep depths of the bridge open out into high walls and a stretch of narrow grey water. Silence. This is another world, on a different level. The streets and busy shops of Kidderminster are left behind. They no longer exist to the traveller down here on the canal. Only a distant hum of machinery is left as a reminder to what lies above. One is not part of the town. It is strange to find such a contrast of worlds lying so close to each other. The canal carries its own world, its own noise and time within itself. The town seems like a world away in its busy present state, and the traveller on this backwater of time is detached from it.

The main feature of the canal is of course the locks. The heavy gates are old, slimy and covered with a lot of green stuff that has thrust itself into the cracks. When the boat goes down and one sits at the front, one can experience a curious sensation.

As the paddles are unwound, the water rushes out and the black slimy walls begin to close in while at the same time the gates tower above. Like a slow lift, the boat sinks and prepares to meet the lower level. As the huge gates open, the new scene is revealed and beckons the boat on to further adventures.

Sometimes locks are set before bridges and this also can be curious for when the gates swing open here, a shallow hole is seen gaping to receive the boat. The towpath runs along the canal side and the workers of the paddles must rush to catch the fleeing boat.

But these canal locks are extremely different from the river locks found on the Severn.

The Day of The Severn

Arriving at Worcester, we now travelled the Severn. The change could be seen from the basin where boats grew into lofty giants of the waterways. Our seventy foot steel monster, with her flapping green canvas, had been the biggest boat on the canal, hugging the bank sides, but now the river sides fell away into the remote distance. Speed was quicker and the wind shrieked in our faces. With a rush we sailed our faithful old barge up the wondrous river.

But the locks were breath-taking. Gigantic twin gates were ready to open at the touch of an electric button, operated by a man in his glass cubical. Lights of red and green gave the signal to advance or halt. Many boats could ride snuggled together to the lower levels. Gates open at the other end by another precise electric button and the boats were free again to prowl the expanse of frothy water.

On and on to the proud towers of Worcester and the majestic cathedral. Dark green trees bushed round its feet and clean grey buildings lined each side. Here was a royal city indeed and rich in noble history. Yet soon Worcester and its busy river are left behind.

***

Back on the canal the journey continues like a dream and unlike the river, the canal carries its own mood. One drifts timelessly over the land, carried by arched aqueducts. Houses, land, roads, are all passed by hundreds of feet below. Then as we travel further on we see bridges pace and span across the water from tree top to tree top. The boat slides under a rusty twirled bridge here, and an eighteenth century one there, the latter standing high to the tops of the trees, draped in clusters of ivy. Like a picture from a painting it stands so peacefully.

Bridges span the murky waters
Looping themselves over reeds bristling with moorhens
And water weighed down with weed and mud
Luscious is it that slurps against the boat sides
Green stuff covers the water like skin
And the boat ploughs through
Leaving a wake like that of an ice-breaker
A black crack down the green channel behind.
On and on
Over aqueduct quietly slipping
Past the men with rods a fishing
Nestled tight between the banks
One is safe to mood and brood
And be teased by dreamy sleep.

The hot sun beats down and the only noise is the hum of the engine. Steer the long boat round the whispering corners and listen to its worn old tune as it chugs down between stone banks. Passing through the silent hoops of bridges like a well aimed croquet ball with only the comforting throb of the engine propelling us through, its echo bouncing off the walls, catching the archway from its sturdy sleep and slinging it into wakefulness. Vibrations of the rattling engine is magnified, circle upon circle, flooding and expanding the expectant air … until … returning the still shouting stones back into their steady slumber, the engine resumes its ceaseless throbbing.

The Day of the Fisherman

On this day there was a competition and fishermen lined the bank with their fishing tackle and gear and large green umbrellas. Round every corner they sat on stools and pointed their slender rigid rods over the waving water. Coloured floats bobbed on the surface and an air of patient waiting surrounded the brightly clad figures. Some were extremely smart, others wore tatty old clothes accompanied by felt hats, while others dressed in neck-to-toe waterproofs, and yet others were in thick sweaters and warm trousers.

Silent in thought, some would raise annoyed eyes at the sound of our boat. Some would shout a comment and others just sighed. Seeing our dramatic approach as we squeezed through locks and bumped banks, some hurriedly drew in their lines and waited until the boat had gone by.

But as the day wore on the fishermen line stretched on too, grouped between the locks and beside the trees. The day became thicker and duller and rain clouds gather across the sky. Slowly but surely these clouds drew together until the sky was full of rain. Everywhere became drab and grey. The dirty canal water snaked off into the leaden hills and the now blackened trees stood on solitary guard in deserted pastures. The rain fell heavily, it's weight dimpling the water with darts, splashing onto the boat making the wood blush a deeper hue. The world looked a dismal place. Then, out of this, loomed a building. It tottered towards the canal leaning from the left bank. A deserted factory.

Such a strange, desolate place
Darkening the horizon.
Once, its mighty wheels turned in work.
Now, they lie rusted and forgotten.
All that is left is the shell,
The husk – open to the skies.
Blank, empty windows gaze over the water
Like huge eye sockets.
All buzz of work life long gone.
Now only the boats drifting by
It stands alone, dirt-grey and ugly.
A place waiting
For the fingers of green piercing nature
To crumble its leaden brick.
Hushed, it towers down, discolouring the water
Quietly forgotten in this backwater
And left for the sighing wind to murmur through.

The Day of Locks and Reservoirs

One day consisted of nothing but locks, steps rising up the hill in a black and white barred procession. Between each was a weedy pool with fishermen on one bank and flat fields on the other. We started in the early haze of morning but it took until midday before the ascent was finished. Through the gates – unwind, shut the gates, wind up, through the next gates and so on, up and through, up and through and the occasional bridge wedged in between was the only thing to break the monotony.

At last the country around began to slope away, undulating smoothly down to the valley in the lazy early sunshine. A peace from an ancient time seems to settle on every hedge and farm stead. Some distance away stood Bromsgrove.

Imagine a twelve century England with travelling tinkers and the noise of wagons rolling over the uneven roads. Musicians singing along the way to the next court, while knights and their ladies ride laughing down the hills among the darkly thrown shadows. They make their way to warm houses with busy smoking chimneys. Rosy cheeked women stand in doorways rubbing floury hands on coarse brown aprons, and mangy dogs pound after the horses keeping a look out for scraps of food. Perhaps also a servant boy runs quickly past dodging through horses on an errand for his lord. Yet it seems the peace now is the essence of the time then. How slow and rural the life must have been. Time to feel part of the wild elements of soil, grass and wind and to turn one's life in time with the turning seasons.

On continued the stepping locks and the barge in her element plunges through each one. Then the reservoirs began to dominate the scenery. One of these was large and peaceful. Across its smooth waters could be seen the trees that framed it. Trees that one thought could never exist except in an eighteenth century landscape, every fine detail picked out by their silvery colour. Their roots spread out to drink at the water's edge, twisted in strange and gnarled shapes. Their leaves were quite still for there was no wind. Only hot morning sunshine beat down upon the delicate branches and upon the glassy water mirroring leafy reflections.

Again a certain time had been caught in one place and held there for a fragile transparent moment.

But this day was a long day for travelling up the Stratford canal. Soon the sun begins to crawl down the paling sky. Light blue turns to darker hue and lights begin to twinkle near and far. A star appears and then another. The sun stretches out its arms and the sky turns violently crimson blended with orange, pink and a deep mauve. Black silhouetted trees stand tall and contrasting to this vivid backdrop. Gradually as the sun sinks further over the sleeping horizon, dark blues, violets and purples splatter the sky and leave a faint blue smudge in the high most points of the sky. Soon the sun, with its veils of clouds is gone and leaves the deep blue and deep grey to shadow the fast darkening countryside. So night descends. Another day passes by, another time, another world, another space.

The Day of Dreaminess

Drifting along on the canal time seems to stand still. Stop and see the flowers on the way, Campion and Wild Rose. Smell the sweet scent as you reach out to pick and crush them in your fingers. Hear the bees droning into flowery landing places and emerge heavy laden with rich yellow pollen. The hedgerow lines the foot path and on the other side, tall yellow-green grasses stand before the rippling waters. The canal winds on by the sheltering hedge, ducking under bridges and throwing itself round corners. Sometimes it is taken over by the reeds and disappears into obscurity but always reappears like an old friend.

All the while the boat glides on the water, gently nuzzles the lock gates and the walker can keep a pace with her slow travel. More flowers bend over and brush their soft petals and leaves against the watery surface and shiver in the breeze. Little trees overhang their branches dropping leaves into the canal as a token of their friendship. Vivaldi's four seasons comes to mind as flowers sway, grasses dance and bees hum in melody flying in the warm breezes.

Suddenly this is all left behind when one goes into a tunnel. One sees the black hole gaping among the green trees at the foot of the hill. As the boat trundles down the straight pathway of the canal, it comes nearer and nearer and then suddenly the boat is chugging into its cold depths. Some tunnels are short and give the impression of extra-long bridges, while others are so long that one is lucky to see a pinpoint of white light at the end indicating the tunnel's furthermost end. The walls are dark and rough but lined with bands of phosphate that pace their way through in archways. Sometimes the roof dips and rises. Occasionally an air vent is revealed, a hole peering down like a black socket through the roof of the tunnel. In a short tunnel one can distinguish its mid-point, by noticing the shades of colour difference between the two openings. The one left behind is butter-yellow but the one in front, draped in trailing creepers, is luscious green.

The end of the tunnel is the most menacing because its reflection is crystal clear in the unmoving water and instead of a semi-circular opening, there is a huge oval shape, ridged like the rib cage of some huge whale. It is like some weird upside-down nightmare. The water being

so clear and still, the boat appears to float on
nothing but air. It hovers in the oval opening
before passing through.

Tales – weaving in and out of
Tunnels – dark and gloomy
Dripping with glistened moisture.
A dark hole stands out midst the wall face
Gaping through the deep green toes of trees.
The mouth of hell is open.
Slow but slow the boat with its rattling engine
Plunges into the dark cold depths therein
And in the far distance is seen the light of
heaven.
Through such hollowed tunnel
White lines of phosphate
Pace the way through.
One by one they leer out of the gloom
And vanish in the ever pursuing gloom
behind.
It is like a ribcage of a whale
And the boat is lured on into the body of the
thing
On and on, on to the beckoning light.

It grows pale then grey then bright
And as suddenly plunged in
The boat is carried out among the trailing
Greenery that loops itself about the brick
And bends over reflected in the clear deep
water.

The Day of Distant Warwick

It is a dull grey day with rain hovering in the chilly air. More sky and trees, more muddy waters and more locks. The day closes in and we travel under the heavy weight of the moody sky. We brood on our black waters listening to Tchaikovsky ringing out his fierce music. Violins and drums rise dramatically to the heights as we sink to the bottom of the locks. Locks with paddles made of black and white stumps with a prong sticking out of the top like a magician's wand.

The darkened locks stretch out, step by step to many towered Warwick. There the city stands peeping from among green layers of trees, stretching into misty distances.

Across the satanic locks that yawn
Into perpetual depths
Stands a steeple
Warwick Cathedral
High above the deepening pale
Shades of trees
There,
It towers.
Scattered on either side and richly framed
By circle upon circle
Of trees holding branches bushed to the skies
And these fringed by hills

Caught in hanging lances of the sun
They surround that lonely steeple.
Back on the still waters of the canal
Water gently laps beneath the bows.
The reeds quiver
And whisper of distant ages echoed at
Warwick castle
Bold lords rustling in their rich brocades
Walked there a courting with their paramours
Light laughter tickles the tiny ripples running
from the bank.
Transparent ghosts caught like particles in a
sunbeam.
The view is the same for centuries still
And little has change from then to now
As the narrow boat passes through.

The grey sky has heralded the coming rain and
now it falls thrashing and lashing the water as it
cascades down. It churns the surface into chaotic
swells and whirlpools.

On the next day Warwick itself is reached. It is
the castle that characterises this ancient place and
throngs of tourists stream between its high walls.
Cameras capture the grace of the windows, the
arch of the door, the twist of the tower and the
squared battlements blasting out their pride over
the plain.

We leave the boat and join the 'Guided Group'
for the grand tour. Now hear the guide in her cut

glass accent ring out the place's condensed historic past. In monotonous drones she recites curtly what she has already said, three times a day, eighteen times a week. Her loud voice rings out over the noise of shuffling feet and muttering tongues. See here the large four poster bed where Elizabeth I slept and look over there at the richly decorated brown and yellow tapestry that adorns the wall. Look up at the ceiling, decked out in little cherubs, sparkling in their golden paint.

We stride in quick succession through the chain of rooms, each more lavish than the one before. No time to listen to the story of the walls or the creak of the oak furniture. We are only strangers, quick to view, quick to pass through and walk away again. What was it like to live and breathe among such ponderous wealth and wear the shining armour that decorates each solemn corner? What skirts rustled down along the wooden floors, and what hushed voices whispered behind closed doors? Most is hidden or forgotten. An age has been and gone and times move on into other times.

The next day the old coal canal boat cleaves the water aside between the Brauston's banks. We dock where we started off and our journey is now at an end. From the tranquil waters of the winding slow canal, we must pick up normal busy lives again. Yet look back and take a last lingering look at the old canal. For a time we caught a glimpse of something ancient, like the fading ripples on water, once seen but now stilled, the ripple of a memory of a quieter time, the canal's time.

Letters from my Dad

I had a wonderful dad. He was a very quiet, gentle man. Careful and thoughtful, a note that he left for my mum about the central heating sums up a little of his character.

> I thought it better to switch off the central heating which would be off anyhow when you get back and not to switch your bed on. Our financial Director had his electric blanket catch fire last week – fortunately he was in the house.
> Turn on the two switches when you come in and soon things will be back to normal and with luck the house will not have been burnt down.
> Always considerate,
> Dick

In the corner is a little cartoon picture of Tigger. The caption underneath reads,

> "I have had my fish."

It's fitting to end these stories with the animals at the beginning of the book and so we return to the adventures of Henry, Pooky and Tigger.

I have mentioned that I was sent to a boarding school. I was very homesick and I think Dad understood this. Each week, he would write letters to me and tell me all the news about the animals at home. He would also include little sketches and drawings which I loved and some of these are included here. These letters would be typed up on his old fashioned black type writer. It was the sort that had arms that sprang forward to type onto the page and made very satisfying clicking noises. Here are a few examples of those wonderful letters.

10th September 1966

My darling Jane,

I will have to type my letters because you would never be able to read my writing and also you get a bit more for your money because I can type faster than I can write.

Tigger is missing you. She is hiding behind her door and dashing out as soon as we open it to look for you. Pooky is eyeing her hungrily and made a snap at her yesterday.

The fish are thriving. Whenever anyone goes near the pond now they think they are going to be fed and follow the person round the pond in a fishy procession. The little ones are not as sensible about this as the bigger ones and they don't know yet which side their bread is buttered.

24th September 1966

Tigger is very full of beans and loves playing by charging flat out round the lounge at terrific speed without ever touching the floor it seems. She can do some prodigious leaping and always lands in the right place.

Pook had a real snap at Tigger and frightened her. I am afraid they will never be good friends. Perhaps it is not very natural for a dog like Pook and a cat like Tigger to be friendly but they have kissed noses.

Henry saw a pussy cat on the wall this morning so what did he do, but put his head back and howled. I have never heard such a noise. The cat looked most amazed.

26th November 1966

Tigger and I have fallen out. She will take a run into the craft room, rush up the screen and suddenly emerge on the top. The only trouble is that the screen is getting scratched and worn. There seems to be something attractive to a pussy cat about rushing up and down screens.

10th December 1966

This is the last letter you should get from me this term because you have only one week to go. Hurrah! Hurrah.!' (sorry the . and the ' got out of line there). I have a Christmas present from Uncle Peter for you and Pook says he would buy you a present if he had any money but he has spent it all on bones.

Today was very wet to begin with and then sunny. Tigger walked down the garden and balanced on the netting on the edge of the pond like the man on the flying trapeze. She dabbled her paws in the water and we all thought we were going to see the first swimming cat.

19th February 1967

Today has been a cold, wet and blustery day. All Tigger's fur was blown up on end and Henry's tail was streaming behind him in the wind.

22nd April 1967

Tigger is missing you, at least she is showing more affection for me so she must be missing you – or it may be because Mum goes out to so many meetings, Parish Councils, Church Councils etc. Recently I have had to get my own tea as often as not.

Pook came in tired and worn out this afternoon after a Tigger hunt round and round the garden – no wonder he was worn out because Tigger was in the house the whole time curled up in a chair fast asleep.

When Mum was out this afternoon at a church sale I got out the ladder and painted the gutter of the garage. Pook looked on apprehensively in case I fell off. I rather damaged some of Mum's plants so I had to go round with the hoe afterwards to straighten things up so that she wouldn't notice.

6th May 1967

Joe the gardener came this morning. Pook stood in the middle of a bed of Snapdragons and wagged his tail at him. Joe refused to notice him. What a way to greet a gardener by standing in the middle of a newly planted flower bed!

The fish are fit and multiplying exceedingly. Eve is being chased all around the pond by her admirers and would-be-wooers. She is very big and obviously preggers. It looks as if we will have masses of little happy events all over the place as last year.

Today I started mowing but ran out of petrol so the front lawn looks as if it is recovering from a thick night and is very ragged.

This morning I tried to play golf but lost four balls. Last Saturday I tried to play but lost three. I have only got two new balls left now. I also lost my temper several times.

Pook had a confrontation with Tigger yesterday. It all goes well until Tigger starts to run away and then Pook cannot resist running after her – usually behind the hedge. I wish they would kiss and be friends.

17th September 1967

Henry is leading Pook a dog's life, pushing him around, biting his ears and generally giving him no peace. Periodically there comes an agonised squeak from the bundle of dogs – but one can never be quite sure which dog it is coming from. If things get too bad, Pooky dives for the armchair. However Henry is undercutting him on this by pulling all the stuffing out.

We are getting on very fast with the new place at the bottom of the garden which Mum has thought up. Most of the digging has been done and it will soon be ready for paving. We can sit down there in the summer and nobody will ever find us.

1st October 1967

Henry fell in the pond. He came out all bedraggled and in a heck of a mess. He overbalanced on the wire netting and joined the fish who were very startled and thought the pond was a little small to hold a whale!

We have finished 'Pleasant Place' at the bottom of the garden just below the pond. It only needs the concreting to be done which depends upon my having the time to get it.

Henry dug a hole in the front lawn and tried to bury a piece of concrete in it which he thought was a bone. I threw the piece of concrete away and he has been giving me disgusted looks ever since.

5th November 1967

It has rained and rained and rained. The lobby and the kitchen are covered in little wet doggy footprints intermingled with big doggy footprints. Tigger has been wet through and came in soaking to the touch. The only happy ones are the fish who must have got a bigger and deeper pond to play in. In fact I expect very shortly they will be swimming up and down the steps into the pleasant place at the bottom of the garden, which is probably half full of water already.

12th November 1967

Henry and Pook and I played ball yesterday. Henry is much faster than Pook but Pook scuttles along with his little legs moving so fast on his round fat body that you can't see them. He uses his head and cuts off the corners so that he sometimes gets the ball before Henry although he can't run as fast.

Henry has dug a huge hole in the front garden in the flower bed adjoining the lawn.

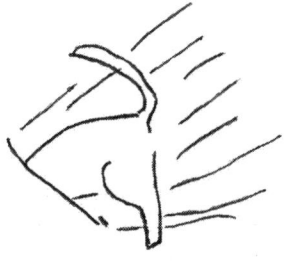

He has dug it four times! Three times we have filled it in and as soon as our back has been turned he has dug it up again – bulbs and all. Pook has wagged the back half of himself ingratiatingly and protested that he had nothing whatsoever to do with the matter which indeed was the case.

19th November 1967

Tigger has been having great fun. The pond was frozen over and this was so new to her that she would chase across it and slide to the other side. I could see her from the bedroom window running flat out on the ice and making no progress whatsoever because her feet were slipping at every stride. The fish were watching her open mouthed from below the ice as she gambolled about above their heads.

It really has been cold and there has been a thick rime of frost on everything when we woke up in the morning.

Henry has been distressingly bouncy. He keeps laddering Mum's stockings so she has to go into trousers in self-defence. He sits on Pook so that the poor little animal can only breathe in grasps. Altogether in every way Henry is making his weight felt! Somehow or other he will have to be unbounced.

November 1967

Henry and Pooky have been thoroughly enjoying themselves barking and baying at the gate till they have nearly driven me nuts stuck up in my study trying to write. Tigger is much more peaceful to live with.

Now Henry has lost his ball and you have never seen such a demented animal. He is completely at sea without it and expects me to produce it for him, quite forgetting that he is the hound and it is up to him to seek things.

3rd December 1967

How are you? As we haven't heard from you this week and you were not so good last Saturday, we are wondering whether you are tucked away in bed with only your nose showing or whether you are still staggering around grinning and bearing it, or are now quite well thank you.

Pooky is now shaped like a barrel with four legs, a tail and head sticking out. His skin is as tight as a drum round an absolutely cylindrical piece of Pook and if you roll him about, provided you stick his legs in he will roll for ever like a barrel rolling down-hill.

10th December 1967

Henry in the snow is a sight for anybody. He was a little doubtful at first but after a bit he realised it was one glorious play-ground. He rushed about throwing it all over the place like a wild cat snow plough. He rolled Pooky over and over in it until he emerged like a polar bear with ginger whiskers. He then chased round and round the garden until the whole place was covered in big, wodgy footprints and one thought an army had been there.

Tigger has enjoyed it too but has come in rather damp and cold with her fur sticking up and has to rush to the nearest radiator to thaw out. However her fur coat has stood her in good stead.

We have had to make little breathing holes for the fish though they were nowhere to be seen and the ice is three inches deep. I expect they are all tucked up in their bed of weeds and very sensibly fast asleep until the thaw.

20th January 1968

Henry is inexhaustible. He goes for long walks and comes home and goes straight for his ball and expects it to be thrown all over the lawn for him. Not so Pooky, he comes home from a walk with a muddy damp undercarriage and just flops on his bed and doesn't expect to be called for a week. Last time I took him for a walk he came home on a sort of stop/start basis by sitting down every hundred yards and asking to be carried. Pooky doesn't seem to get any thinner by walking.

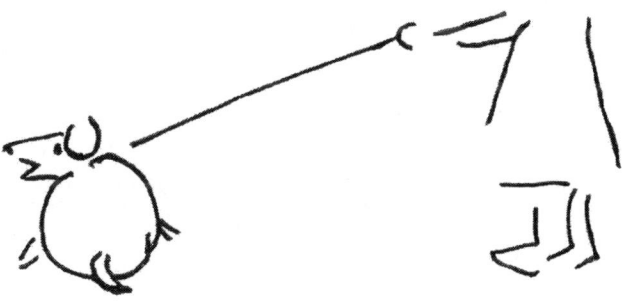

Mum says she has written to you about your behaviour in house. We understand that lots of the girls were much worse. However try to get better reports both in the house and in school work because it is a waste of a good opportunity if you don't.

28th January 1968

A fine day today and as I thought would happen pretty soon Henry got his nose caught in the fridge whenever the door is open. So after due warning I shut the door and his nose was still in it – it's alright – it didn't hurt him – just a warning that's all.

The other day he insisted on sticking his nose in the oven and wuffling at the joint. We warned him it was hot but he still stuck it in and then got a blast of hot air up each nostril which he brought back and blew out at me like a dragon.

Pooky is a most polite little dog. He asks permission to go out and be sick when his breakfast is delayed. He is most apologetic about it. "But Master, if my breakfast isn't ready with your kind permission I must forthwith withdraw to be sick."

The fish are coming out of their winter hibernation. Only the big ones have appeared so far. I hope they haven't eaten up all the little ones.

That Henry! He simply loves sliding down the coal heap and pulling all the coal out of the coal shed onto the ground round about and I have to then pick it up. What a 'orrible 'ound.

25th May 1968

Pooky is quite comatose (that means fat and placid!). He is a bundle of fur and badly needs a haircut. It is so ridiculous, his hair is growing in waves, at least he doesn't need a perm and set.

Tigger comes rushing when I call her in in the evening. Sometimes she sneaks up behind me and stands by my side staring out into the garden as I shout "Tigger!" You can almost feel that she is trying to shout "Tigger" too.

8th June 1968

Henry is in disgrace, he will jump up at people and wuffle up ladies' skirts and he will not take "no" for an answer. Mum got very cross with him, she wanted to cuddle Pook but of course that wouldn't suit Henry as he wanted to be in on the act. In the end she had to tell him that he was a disagreeable dog but he thought that was a term of endearment and he wuffled up all the closer.

I haven't seen Tigger for two days, she comes in for her eats but spends the rest of the time happily wandering round the garden and jumping up at the butterflies.

Mum is weeding the front garden but this is a bit of a dead loss as a big footed gentleman very soon goes and puts his big feet plumb on the middle of the beds which is a little disheartening. I must go and join her and do some mowing.

June 1968

Henry's hole, this gets bigger every day. It is no earthly use filling it in again because he just digs it up and scatters bulbs all over the place. Mum is cross with him, Joe the gardener won't talk to him and so it all goes on. Henry is the only one who looks happy about it.

We had a lovely mummy hedgehog in the garden the other evening. We watched it through the window drinking milk from a saucer. Tigger was scared stiff of it and wouldn't go within two feet. It washed the milk down with some water from the pond and then went to sleep on the concrete by the edge of the pond.

22nd June 1968

Today it has just rained and rained and rained. Henry and Pooky have done nothing except sit huddled up together in the armchair. However Henry has done more than that, he has tried to pull the armchair to pieces. I expect by the time you come home it will only be four legs standing on the floor with Henry sitting happily in the middle having eaten the rest.

Tigger is not happy about the weather either, although she has had her garden door open most of the day she has hesitated to go out and prefers sitting snug in a corner.

Sometime between July and September 1968

Bark! Bark!! Bark!!! Why do they always have to wait till I am writing letters in my room and trying to concentrate to decide that it is time to raise the neighbourhood. It's never anything very important either – just a little matter of being brave when you are the right side of the gate.

24ᵗʰ November 1968

Oh what a horrible smell! I'm afraid something has died in the house, probably under the floor boards in my room. We have to keep all the windows open to let the pong out. We have had it about four times before. Last time it was in the dining room. We took all the floor boards up and found the tiniest little dead mouse about two inches long and the smell had been enough nearly to drive us out of the house. After a bit the corpses dry up and the smell disappears.

Only three weeks to go now to the end of term and then it will be Christmas and cometh Uncle Charles and all sorts of good things. I have to give up my room to Uncle Charles*. He can have it at the moment, pong and all and good luck.

1st December 1968

The 'pong' is still with me but provided I keep the window open most of the time I don't notice it. Tigger is very thrilled about the smell of dead mouse and has been paying me visits, rubbing herself round my legs. It looks as if she feels that I am the donor of dead-mouse smell. I wish I could give it away.

19th January 1969

Yesterday it blew and rained and the river was up in floods over the road. Today is a lovely day with the sun shining, snowdrops coming out in the garden and the river is its normal self again. If it keeps like it is today for a period it will soon be spring.

*I have to mention here a note about Uncle Charles. He was my Dad's cousin and Dad could not stand him. Yet every Christmas Mum insisted we had to have Uncle Charles to stay. He lived on his own, had never married and was a bit odd.

Pooky gets younger everyday now he has lost his excessive weight and he gambols about like a two year old.

Henry has chewed my spectacle case. He spat the spectacles out fortunately without breaking them, so he is in disgrace.

I can smell lunch a-brewing up so must finish now.

26th January 1969

Today is spring like. Henry is showing his spring fever by first of all running figures of eight all over the lawn and secondly bouncing up and down on his hind legs at the gate with his head back and baying at any unfortunate passer-by, human or dog. This all contributes to the peace and quiet of a village Sunday morning.

Sometime in the summer 1969

We had the most colossal storm at work on Thursday, it was just as if someone had tipped up a huge bath, huge hailstones as well. Of course all the traffic was paralysed and everybody started to run into each other. A gentleman walked into my office with a door handle and said he had knocked it off somebody's car. I didn't try to go home until six o'clock.

22nd February 1970

I have a nasty sore throat so you had better hold this letter at arm's length, don't breathe in when reading it and burn it afterwards. It may be infectious and be carried like the plague of London (to strike a historical GCE note).

On Friday Henry walked Mum completely off her feet. Henry if you please was so full of energy that when he came back he had to rush round on the lawn, charging in and out of the kitchen and sending Pooky rolling over and over. We told him he was supposed to be tired but it had no effect.

Next day the cat went mad and pretended it was a wild cat, put its ears back and charged vertically up the curtains. Perhaps it was a first touch of spring but our animals seemed badly touched. Pooky slept through it all as usual even when he was rolled over he came out sleeping.

Sometime between March and April !1970

The other day we had thunder and lightning. Then Mum heard an awful commotion. Henry was howling som'at cruel and when she went to investigate she found the inevitable Pook stuck in the gate and she had to push and prod him until he was free.

It is about to rain so I must continue with my painting quickly before it does. It is now the next morning and Mum arrived home at the end of the last paragraph.

5th June 1970

Very hot here again today and Mum has had another attack of the vapours or whatever it is called when you do excessive gardening in the heat of the afternoon and have to lie down in the shade drinking cool lemonade and looking hot and bothered.

Henry and Pook also sit down in the middle of the hot lawn and are too heat-weary to get up and bark when a convoy of small children, normally a Henry admiration society, tacks curiously past the gate. However a Boxer on a taut lead suspended from a small girl was really too much for Henry and he gave terrible tongue, it sounded like the voice of doom.

12th September 1970

I gather your room is a bit rough and they still have the numbers on the doors as when it was a hotel. My comment on that is that they have the same system in prisons.

Pooky as you probably know has been plucked, or not only plucked but almost shaven. He looks not so much like a spring lamb but a middle aged gentleman in his altogethers, which there is no sight so unattractive. But at least his red hair is now sprouting through unhindered by the old wool and also has even growth all over including the previous bald patches.

I have suggested to Mum that she tries the same principle on me so when next you see me I may be bald headed but have a lovely crop of new red hair sprouting up.

20th September 1970

Pooky is an entirely new dog. He is now covered in fresh red short hair, even his tail is growing. He is as frisky as anything, his old weight of decaying fur had been evidently too much for him.

Unfortunately he can now squeeze through the gates. Mr Smith has brought him back twice from the Mill. Mum had to put wire netting on the iron gate. Yesterday he got stuck three-quarters the way through. From the garage he only appeared to have a front half as his last quarter was wedged, his tail was free and wagged it apologetically. Henry was barking excitedly.

I had to make a decision as to whether to pull him forwards or push him backwards. I decided to do the first and got him through tucking in legs and tails and other little bits and pieces which we men understand.

October 1970

Henry met Trudy for the first time half an hour ago nose to nose. After the usual courtesies Trudy wished to make further advances at which Henry put his tail between his legs and ran for his life although he was far the bigger dog. He is not terribly brave.

21st November 1970

Mrs Collins rang up last night to ask if we had lost Henry as she had seen a Bassett Hound wandering about. We checked in the kitchen and there sat Henry so we referred her to the Bowdons and hoped they hadn't lost Trudy. There are one or two Beagles about which could be mistaken for Bassets in the dark.

We think something has died again under the boards in my bedroom. The upstairs smells like a corpse and I can hardly bare to have the window closed. This usually happens before Charles comes but he doesn't seem to notice the smell.

Tigger is lonely, we think we will have to have her psycho-analysed. She even follows me around devotedly, perhaps she does need her head examining.

The pond fountain is all finished. We can switch the fountain on with a flick of a switch from indoors. The fish are very impressed.

Sometime before Christmas 1970
Henry ate a cactus! It was one Mum had put out ready for Christmas. Why it was within reach is not quite clear but perhaps Mum thought it was immune.

Henry is like a goat or a donkey, he will eat anything and we thought of giving him a good bowl of nettles, dandelions or thistles for his supper. The inevitable happened and he was ignominiously sick in a corner of the kitchen.

21st March 1971

Yesterday there was a most appalling screeching and carrying on outside on the terrace. Mum rushed out to find a full blooded cat fight in process. The black and white stray was fighting Ginger for possession of the terrace which didn't belong to either of them. Fur was coming out in handfuls and the whole terrace was covered in ginger fur. Tigger was refereeing and joining in at intervals but only by way of an occasional pat with both paws as if to say, "Stop it! Don't behave like that on my territory." We had to shoo the whole lot away.

26ᵗʰ June 1971

It is Tigger's turn to be in trouble this week. Mum had all the cakes laid out in the dining room ready for the church fete the next day. Unfortunately the door had been left open and Tigger managed to sneak in and ate the 'o' out of the word orange on Mum's orange cake. She did it very neatly but Mum had no more orange icing to put in its place. I expect it finished up sort of pie-bald.

4ᵗʰ July 1971

The new grass is growing apace and we will soon be able to lie on the lawn and watch the fish in the pond and the fountain at play except that it won't play at the moment because its bunged up with weeds. Tigger insists on rolling on the new grass so it will have little hollows in it where she has rolled.

Henry likes sitting on the lawn in the front garden but doesn't see why he shouldn't be allowed into the back garden as well. He doesn't appreciate the fact that it will go to his head and he would run amok among the cabbages.

Sometime over the summer 1971

I am in a bad temper. It is raining which is bad at any time and doubly bad on a Saturday. Henry wet the floor again, Mum's electric stove has packed up, she has lost a diamond out of her engagement ring and the knob dropped off the toaster. All this as if I didn't have enough to do at the weekends anyhow! Henry is still in disgrace.

Sometime over the summer 1971

At last yesterday I have virtually finished painting the gate. Henry celebrated the fact by snuffling at it and getting white paint all over his nose. The cat next will walk along the top leaving little black foot prints. I know them.

Trudy poked her head through the gate today and Henry was very pleased to see her. Evidently she comes to pay her respects at least once a day. It is the wrong way round to do courting but perhaps things are different with dogs and anyhow she has always been the more forward and Henry maidenly more bashful!

And finally I include a piece of writing from my Dad about the wonderful Henry. As I read it I cried with laughter and I hope it will make you laugh too.

With the author's compliments.

Henry by Richard Charlesworth

He was clearly a hound but his skin was soft and floppy and he had the biggest feet and eyes of any puppy we had seen. His ears trailed on the ground and if he accidently trod on them he found himself pinned down unable to move. He was a bundle of slobbering affection and we just had to have him.

Getting him home was just not so easy. We prophesied he would be carsick and he certainly was – within the first half mile. This continued at intervals throughout the journey. He insisted on sitting on everyone's lap and licking their faces. He still insists on doing this even though three times the size.

Naming him presented a problem too. We searched Surtees for hound like names but somehow Jasper or Bluebell did not seem suitable. Fred had been monopolised by another very famous dog of his breed. At length we struck on the simple name of Henry and Henry he became.

Soon the whole village knew him. Small boys going home from school would peer through the gate calling him by name. he developed a fan club. Lurching through the village he would meet many friends whom we did not know but he was always pleased to see them and pass the time of day.

We had another dog, a wire haired dachshund by the name of Pookers. Henry immediately took to him as a fellow in need, but did anyone dare make a fuss of Pookers and Henry intervened himself straightaway, insisting that he be the centre of the party. Poor Pookers (he suffered amongst other things from chronic halitosis) – and his legs were short – he was constantly bowled over by the much larger Henry, but rolling himself over once or twice like a ball he soon recovered and was ready for more of the same treatment.

Romance came into Henry's life when he met Trudy, a Bassett bitch who lived round the corner. Thereafter Trudy would not pass the gate without seeing if Henry was at home. He generally was and very friendly too behind the bars of the gate. If he met Trudy out for a walk he rushed away from her, straining to the end of his lead, a terrible coward, the very antithesis of masculine virility.

Then there was the time he came out in lumps – it seems that Bassetts are prone to them. One came up on his head and we expected to see a daffodil sprout out of it. It had to be removed. Another came up on his bottom near his tail and that had to be removed as well – and so it went on. Finally three had to be removed at once. Each time he had to wear a cardboard collar to prevent his pulling out the stitches and he wandered about, smelling of ether and looking more and more like a clown out of a pantomime.

He had a canvas bed but it wore down to the ground and became dirty and old so we bought him a brand new basket, the biggest and best in the shop. We brought it home proudly but Henry refused to sit in it, surveying it suspiciously from outside. My wife had to sit in it to show him what it was for and he nestled up to her comfortably enough but it was a long time before he would use it on his own.

Now he is a veteran, greying at the muzzle but still accepted by everyone. He uses the chairs in the lounge as his right and privilege. He can be an infernal nuisance at times because his feet will get in the way and being stumpy in the leg he has never lost the habit of jumping up. In exasperation my elder daughter once exclaimed "I don't love Henry any more" but one look form his brown eyes and she had to admit that really she still did.

He is well established now as the best known dog in the village.

Conclusion

There are many more stories that could be included. There is the one about Flute, my sister's tame thrush. It was rescued and lived with us for a while until one day it just flew off, healthy and free again. Or I could tell about my sister's geese. She kept them for several years. One of them, Trousers, was a bit vicious. I am afraid he ended up for Christmas dinner, a bit sad really.

Animals will always be with us and share our lives. Capture and treasure the moments wherever you find them. Hopefully these stories recorded here have made you chuckle and smile.

Acknowledgements

A big thank you to all the following people;
Jane Leversha-Morris, Scott Hutchinson, Sally
Appleby, Uncle Freddie for the story about Patch,
John Hayter for his Raven and Kipper Pie Story,
Yvonne Wood for her Chicken Story, and Eileen
Smith for proofreading.

Thank you to Nick, my husband, for his
patience and help with the final proofreading.

Also thank you to family and friends that have
made these stories possible.

Henry and Tigger

Tigger

Auntie Eileen and Patch

Dick (my dad) with Meg's puppies

Leo the great hunter

Meg as a kitten

Felix the Escape Artist

The author and Henry

Other books by the author

Sister Sunshine

A wartime romance about the author's Mum.

Joy was a nurse during WW2 and was there when Vesuvius erupted. She married Tony Case her sweetheart in Algiers, North Africa and they served together in Italy.

A beautiful story which became the adventure of a lifetime.

Available on Amazon

Printed in Great
Britain
by Amazon